Jack
Longstreet

Books by Sally Zanjani

The Unspiked Rail:
Memoir of a Nevada Rebel

The Ignoble Conspiracy:
Radicalism on Trial in Nevada

Jack Longstreet:
Last of the Desert Frontiersmen

Goldfield:
The Last Gold Rush on the Western Frontier

Jack Longstreet

Last of the Desert Frontiersmen

by Sally Zanjani

University of Nevada Press
Reno Las Vegas London

VINTAGE WEST SERIES
SERIES EDITOR: ROBERT E. BLESSE

A list of books in the series appears at the end of this volume.

Jack Longstreet: Last of the Desert Frontiersmen was first published by Swallow Press/Ohio University Press in 1988. The 1994 University of Nevada Press edition reproduces the original except for the front matter, which has been modified to reflect the new publisher, and a new cover design.

Cover photo of Jack Longstreet, courtesy of Nevada State Museum and Historical Society, Las Vegas. Cover photo of horse race, courtesy of Jim Wolfe Collection, Central Nevada Historical Society, Tonopah.

The paper used in this book meets the requirements of American National Standard for Information Sciences—Permanence of Paper for Printed Library Materials, ANSI Z39.48-1984. Binding materials were selected for strength and durability.

LIBRARY OF CONGRESS CATALOGING-IN-PUBLICATION DATA

Zanjani, Sally Springmeyer, 1937-
Jack Longstreet : last of the desert frontiersmen / Sally Zanjani.
p.   cm.   —(Vintage West series)
ISBN 0-87417-236-5 (paperback : alk. paper)
1. Longstreet, Andrew Jackson, b. ca. 1834. 2. Pioneers—Nevada—
Biography. 3. Pioneers—Arizona—Biography. 4. Indians of North
America—Southwest, New—History. 5. Frontier and pioneer life—
Nevada. 6. Frontier and pioneer life—Arizona. 7. Nevada—
Biography. 8. Arizona—Biography. I. Title. II. Series.
[F841.L66Z36 1994]   979'.02'092—dc20
[B]   93-39982   CIP

University of Nevada Press, Reno, Nevada 89557 USA
Copyright © 1988 Sally Zanjani. All rights reserved
Cover design by Erin Kirk
Printed in the United States of America

1 3 5 7 9 8 6 4 2

To Esmail, with love

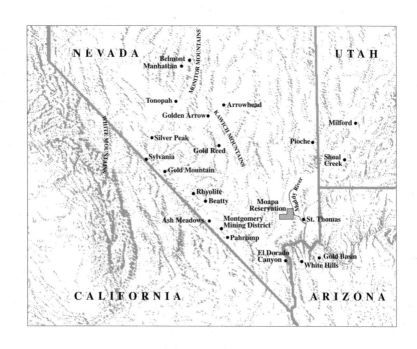

Table of Contents

Acknowledgements

In the course of years of search for the elusive Longstreet, I have accumulated more than an author's usual share of debts. The first is to my father, George Springmeyer, who twenty years after his death remains the intellectual wellspring for my work. The yellowed newspaper clipping on Longstreet found among my father's effects was the origin of this book. Because my father had saved it for nearly forty years, it seemed like a message impregnated with meaning.

As my research progressed, the people who generously shared their time and their memories with me were particularly valuable to the Longstreet story because written sources were often scanty. I am especially grateful to Joseph Clifford, George Ishmael, Alice Lorigan, Olephia King, Austin Wardle, and Sonia DeHart. Material I would otherwise have missed was made available to me through the generosity of several colleagues, Phillip Earl, Richard Lingenfelter, David Millman, Evelyne Wash-Pickett, Guy Rocha, and Maryellen Sadovitch. Other colleagues at the libraries and historical societies where I sought assistance provided much aid and many courtesies. Special mention should be made of Carmelita Ryan, National Archives, Lee Mortensen, Nevada Historical Society, Steven Wood, Utah Historical Society, Donaly Brice, Texas State Archives, Lori Davisson, Arizona Heritage Center, and William Metscher, Central Nevada Historical Society. Denise Moran, Theresa Pate, and Becky Bumguardner, Nye County courthouse, Tonopah, Nevada, and other patient and helpful county officials at numerous Western county courthouses went far beyond the call of duty in responding to my requests for old records. In addition, I am indebted to genealogist Oma Rose, Edward Reed, and several members of the National Outlaw and Lawman History Association for their endeavors to help me solve the mystery of Longstreet's early life. Carrie Porter and Anthony Gidari were kind enough to read and criticize my work. I was also especially fortunate to have the benefit of C. L. Sonnichsen's encouragement and insightful advice on the manuscript.

In a biography of Longstreet, the remote and beautiful desert places where he lived were necessarily an integral part of the story. Some I reached with the help of a worthy successor to the early desert travelers, my oldest son, Don Springmeyer. In Ash Meadows, David Livermore provided helpful advice, and Robert Love was an excellent and knowledgeable guide to people and places in the area. My husband, Esmail, was not only a discerning editor but also an indefatigable companion on many forays into the world beyond the pale. Not the least of my thanks are owed to Keith Boni. Had it not been for his assistance on an unfortunate day in the Kawich, both author and book might have come to an untimely end.

Introduction

"Nevada is one of the very youngest and wildest of the States," wrote John Muir in an essay published in 1879, "nevertheless it is already strewn with ruins that seem as gray and silent and time-worn as if the civilization to which they belonged had perished centuries ago." The deserted Nevada mining camps Muir observed had flourished and died in the span of less than a generation. Only thirty years had passed since the California gold rush unleashed the great migration to the far West. Only twenty years separated the discovery of silver on the Comstock and the exuberant boom that followed from borrasca, depopulation, and the long fruitless search for a new bonanza on the lode. Only fifteen years had passed since the final smolderings of hostilities with the Paiutes were crushed in the aftermath of the Owens River War. In Ash Meadows, on the eastern fringe of Death Valley, Indians were still living—and much in the style of their forefathers—who had shot their arrows at the white invaders.

In 1880, sixteen years after Nevada became a state, it appeared that the inexorable exhaustion of the old mining bonanzas would do what Indian arrows had failed to accomplish. The new white settlers were leaving the land in droves. The already small population of Nevada was to decline over the ensuing twenty years by almost a third from 62,000 in 1880 to 42,000 in 1900. While the largest exodus occurred from Virginia City, the same process was at work in the small but once thriving mining camps of central and southern Nevada. Pioche was sliding into decay, Belmont was about to wither into a village, and Aurora was already a ghost town. The greater part of the state's remaining population was clustered around the Comstock like survivors clinging to a shipwreck, while in the southern 40 percent of the state, occupied by Lincoln, Nye, and Esmeralda counties, there was one person for every seven square miles. Even this statistic was misleading because most people were gathered in mining camps and locales hospitable to ranching, leaving stretches of fully thousands of square miles without a single inhabitant, Indian or white. By 1900 these three counties contained less than 6,500 people in a land area of nearly 46,000 square miles, greater than the size of Connecticut, Delaware, Maryland, New Hampshire, Rhode Island, New Jersey, and Massachusetts combined.

This dominion remained a huge unassimilated lump of the frontier long after the West's more favored climes had grown civilized, because it was a formidable desert with many long dry stretches where the foolhardy perished and the wise traveler passed through as quickly as possible. Actually, the three southern Nevada counties straddle two deserts: the sagebrush desert of the Great Basin, and the hotter Joshua tree and creosote lands of the Mojave to the south, bordering on the baking desolation of Death Valley. In much of the Mojave average annual precipitation varies between four and eight inches and summer temperatures not infrequently rise to 115 or 120 degrees. From the Utah border on the east to the White Mountains on the California border to the west, these deserts are bisected by parallel ranges of mountains running mostly north and south. A number of these chains are by no means inconsequential (Boundary Peak, the highest mountain among them, brushes the clouds at more than 13,000 feet), but the greater barriers to exploration and settlement were the broad, waterless desert valleys of the southern interior. According to pioneer historian Myron Angel, the prospector who ventured into this *terra incognita* was "thought exceeding bold," a view that did not greatly change until after the turn of the century.

The strict limitations imposed upon agriculture by the desert climate barred stockmen from filling the economic breach when the mines of the southern region played out. By 1880 the fragile desert was already showing signs of overgrazing. The white sage that had provided such succulent winter feed for cattle in the valleys of northern Nye County was already stripped, and the oases of deep, lush grasses noted by early travelers had been cropped away. There were other constrictions and setbacks. The ready market of the mining camps that had stimulated ranching during the 1860s had by now evaporated, and stock and produce could not readily be shipped to more distant markets because railroads had penetrated no farther than the fringes of the region. Transportation was still the infrequent stagecoach or, more often, the burro.

A large hiatus in agricultural progress occurred in the 1870s when the industrious Mormons, for reasons of their own, returned to Utah from the Moapa and other southern valleys, leaving their farms to be reclaimed by the sagebrush and the blowing sand. Although these settlers were eventually replaced and the number and value of ranches in southern Nevada as a whole increased substantially in the late nineteenth century, Muir's observation remained as true as when he made it: "Compared with the arid stretches of valley and plain . . . [Nevada ranches] are mere specks lying inconspicuously here and there, in out-of-the-way places, often thirty or forty miles apart."

Sandwiched between the pious, communally organized Mormons to the east and the comfortable, sophisticated California cities to the west, southern Nevada consequently remained an island world where the settling process had scarcely begun and the culture of an earlier day still survived until the turn of the century. Long after the individualistic gold panners of the mother lode country had been replaced by hired miners working regular shifts in absentee-owned industrial enterprises, Montgomery, a small camp on the fringe of the Spring Mountains, overflowed with hopeful prospectors but counted not a single woman in its population—and that was in 1891. The old frontier also lived on in the isolation of pioneer homesteaders separated by a day's ride or more from the sand-roofed cabin of their nearest neighbors. The wife of one such settler greeted every stranger with unmitigated joy, even the county assessor.

The frontier survived, too, in the unmistakable presence of a taciturn kind of man who naturally gravitated to places beyond the realm of the law. It was said at one time that every white man in Ash Meadows was "on the dodge for something," and a study of Bodie, a mining camp just across the Nevada-California border, has shown homicide rates in the 1880's more than three times greater than in any large American city a century later. Finally, the old tradition of the mountain men, many of whom had learned Indian ways, loved Indian women, and moved easily back and forth across the barrier between the Indian and white worlds, remained alive in Ash Meadows, where most white settlers were squaw men who had taken Indian wives.

If there are few men for all seasons and most that tower above the rest are necessarily creatures of their times, displaced in any other, it follows that a hero for this desolate and isolated region would be cast in a mold familiar a generation and more earlier but not much needed since. He would not require the religious vision and the coordinating genius of the leaders of Mormondom to the East. He would have scant use for the ability to organize great mining enterprises and reap millions from the stock market like a John Mackay. Nor would the mustangs and jackrabbits that were the principal inhabitants of southern Nevada in those days provide much scope for a lawyer and opportunist extraordinaire like William Stewart. The qualities that made the lords of busi-

ness and the politicians in the great cities dwindled into ir-
relevance in these perilous deserts, where death lurked in the
hand of a murderous renegade and the parching rays of the
summer sun. In this domain, the survival skills of the first
generation of Western explorers were the only kind that
counted for much.

The man this region demanded would be closer to a Daniel
Boone than to the new mining tycoons, and it would be to his
advantage if he also possessed considerable proficiency with
a gun. It would ease his passage and allow him sounder sleep
beside his campfires by night if he were accepted as one of the
people in the scattered reed huts of the Southern Paiutes. He
would be, in short, a frontier hero.

Our written sagas of the pioneer period suggest that southern Nevada was almost as inhospitable to heroic figures as to
rainfall and to verdant vegetation. An occasional trailblazer
passed through: Jed Smith made a pair of journeys in
1826–1827, losing ten of the eighteen men who accompanied
him on the second in an Indian attack; Joe Walker tried to cut
across the region on his return from California in 1834 but
was forced to turn back toward the Sierra when the thirsty
members of his party rebelled against continuing into the
waterless desert near Death Valley. The experiences of later
emigrants who sometimes strayed too far from established
trails, like the early probings of Smith and Walker, tended to
be quickly transformed into exercises in escape. Yet, as the
first outposts of ranching and the early mining camps
emerged, men began to arrive who sought the remotest
reaches of this last frontier as avidly as their predecessors
had shunned them. Of course they had their reasons, sometimes personal and eccentric, not infrequently pressing and
legal. But it is among their annals rather than in the well-
known sagas of perilous passages that the region's own in-
digenous heroes must be sought.

The human material does not appear overly promising at
first, consisting mostly of prospectors, desperadoes on the

run, and mining magnates who made their bundles and then departed to build their luxurious mansions in the cities by the sea. Nonetheless, one man quickly stands out, one who did his share of prospecting yet exhibited a range of survival skills that separated him from the other prospectors, a man with several notches on his gun and a shadowy past who still did not entirely fit in the rough company of the outlaws, a loner who seemed to belong in a class by himself. The name he went by was Jack Longstreet.

Among the prospectors, it would be difficult to see the small, Chaplinesque figure of Shorty Harris, or any of the rest who meandered endlessly through the sagebrush after their burros, as much more than minor curiosities, though the less reclusive among them delighted in their own reputations. The most assiduous reputation-builder was Death Valley Scotty, who worked for years at fabricating a mystery and a legend around his name. He succeeded little better than he deserved, creating a spectacle that may well have amused a man like Jack Longstreet, who was generally more inclined to duck his legend than to inflate it. Some of these prospectors succumbed to the desert in the end, like old John LeMoigne, who thought forty years of desert journeying had taught him how to cross Death Valley in the summer—and died there all the same. And few approached Longstreet's record of half a century of survival beyond the pale. Although scholarship has designated 1890 as the year that marks the closing of the frontier, it is important to remember that when Longstreet was ranching on his Oasis Valley homestead in that year he was one of only three white men in seven thousand square miles, a great part of which was designated the Unexplored Desert and was not even completely mapped for more than fifteen years.

Although Longstreet prospected and mined off and on for half a century, he was hardly a picturesque and harmless old prospector on the order of Harris or LeMoigne. By the same token, he was not quite the same as the other desperadoes hiding in the region. When he is compared with a man like Dave Neagle, who was perhaps the best known of the floating outlaw crew, it is evident that Neagle lacked Longstreet's staying power. The desert was no more than a temporary sanctuary for Neagle, from which he moved on to his future career as gunman and sometime lawman in Bodie, Tombstone, Butte, and finally California. By contrast, Longstreet remained, frequently on the move, of course, but nearly always somewhere within the area of northwestern Arizona and southcentral Nevada.

Moreover, it became clear with the passage of time that people relied on Longstreet in certain situations: when there was a killer to be tracked through country where law officers were afraid to go, when signposts to save lives were needed in a desert that only one white man knew well enough to mark. At these junctures Neagle and his kind were generally long gone, and it was to Longstreet that county authorities turned when they needed someone who rode the unmapped wastes as easily as others boarded a train, spoke with the Indians in their own language, and was never known to shrink from confrontation. Finally, there is no sign that the Neagles ever fought for any larger concern than professional duty or personal gain, while Longstreet's protest against the ill treatment of the Indians at the Moapa Reservation suggests that perhaps he did.

Out in Longstreet's part of the world, he was easily recognized as a frontier hero, an impression to which the panache of his appearance contributed. Even in his late seventies, he still stood nearly six feet tall and straight "as a sequoia," as newspaper reporters were apt to say when they described him. His powerful, broad-shouldered build made him seem even taller. His sparkling blue eyes were a startling contrast to his ruddy skin, tanned almost as dark as an Indian's, and the long white hair that concealed his mysterious cropped ear. His striking appearance was enhanced by a soft Southern drawl, a gentlemanly, almost courtly, style, and a warm brand of Southern hospitality that offered every amenity to a guest (and a cocked gun to the unidentified stranger). All this, coupled with Longstreet's ability to read and write reasonably well for someone raised on the frontier in his generation, lent support to the popular belief that he was not just another tough hombre but a man of gentle birth, indeed a close connection of the Confederate general, James Longstreet, and the Southern aristocracy.

The men of Longstreet's day respected his extraordinary prowess with the long-barreled Colt. 44 preferred by the old-time gunfighters, yet they distinguished him from that criminal underclass, often gamblers and sometimes thieves, to which many gunmen clearly belonged. This was largely because Longstreet met an unwritten but well-understood code of conduct. Although none of Longstreet's gunfights conformed to that classic duel in the sun at high noon in which two men pace toward each other down the street and the fastest draw wins, neither did most frontier affrays. Close scrutiny has shown, for example, that Wild Bill Hickok's famous battle with a large gang of raiders at Rock Creek Station, actually consisted of Hickok and his companions killing three unarmed farmers.

It was reality of this variety, rather than the fantasies of dime novels, that had shaped the expectations of most of Longstreet's acquaintances. While a man was not expected to vanquish an army singlehandedly or to hold his fire chivalrously under provocation, he was expected to avoid shedding innocent blood. On this basis, Longstreet's killings were considered justified on grounds of self-defense. No one had ever seen him strutting at gunplay for display or brandishing his gun to intimidate others, though he was capable of subduing someone who did. This, too, was approved. As for the horse thievery that had reputedly earned him his cropped ear, it was dismissed as a youthful escapade in a place and time where mutual horse stealing was so widespread that those caught were more unlucky but not more guilty than the rest.

In these abilities as gunfighter and survivor, as in a great deal else, Longstreet was cut from cloth that Westerners at the turn of the century recognized and, if the truth were said, admired. This old man, who had restlessly roamed the West as the spirit moved him and refused to settle down in pursuit of conventional success, had led a life of which those hobbled by their ambitions and obligations could only dream. He had ventured where few dared to go, and had survived.

Like the great frontier heroes of a generation before him— Sam Houston, Jim Bridger, Joe Walker, and the rest— Longstreet was unmistakably an Indian lover, with his Indian wives, his Indian companions, and his Indian ways. Formally, this was condemned, but underneath the censure Westerners sensed the pull of the wild and dashing way of life of an Indian, who fought for sheer excitement, hunted and explored when it pleased him, danced on the mountaintops, and flung himself into riotous bouts of gambling and drinking with complete abandon. That same magnet had drawn the young Tom Horn west into the mountains of the White River to live with the Apache. No wonder people saw in Longstreet the freedom of the old frontier.

To those who knew him, the preference of an unmistakably dangerous man for the world beyond the pale was its own explanation and the only one that Longstreet was ever likely to give. He kept no journal, left no reminiscence, and never talked much about his past, especially where sensitive matters were concerned. His silence was always respected. Moreover, the records in which he appears are scanty because large portions of his life were spent in remote regions where newspapers did not exist and census takers did not penetrate. Although the combined sources on his career are extensive and satisfactory at some points, they turn fragmentary farther back in time, finally dwindling away entirely in 1879.

One day, in the cracked and aging ledgers of some small county courthouse, the missing clue that would solve the puzzle of his early life may finally come to light. But until then Longstreet must ride into town from nowhere, as in the classic opening scene of a western movie. It is a myth so deeply ingrained in the American consciousness that we know it well—jagged mountains on the horizon, a little desert settlement of adobes, a tall mysterious stranger with a notched gun riding through the dusty street. In the life of Longstreet, however, the myth was also the truth. It is a fitting start for the story of the first and last frontier hero of the Kawich and points south to Ash Meadows and Sylvania, the man of whom so much was said and so little known. We begin with the stranger.

1
El Dorado

The glow of a winter sunset still stained the sky above the black mountains as William Marsh and his friends drove their team into Warnable Springs on a December night in 1900. Their destination lay three miles farther south, a new boom town named Tonopah where silver had recently been discovered. A campfire burned near the spring; beside it crouched a big, powerful man with long hair. In his hands was a rifle. Unable to see the flashing blue of the stranger's eyes in the dim glow of the firelight, Marsh mistook him for an Indian. Cautiously, young Marsh stepped forward to make his explanations.

In all likelihood, the man by the campfire had already decided that Marsh and his companions were harmless or he would have awaited them, as was his custom, on the far side of his horse with a cocked gun. Marsh was allowed to come closer, his account of himself was presently accepted, and from that time forward the man by the campfire and he were "warm friends"—at least Marsh liked to think so. Nonetheless, that friendship was never to grow sufficiently warm to allow Marsh to linger overnight with a herd of sheep at the watering place near Longstreet's cabin.

The true identity of Andrew Jackson ("Jack") Longstreet, the man whom Marsh and many others mistook for an Indian, or perhaps a half-breed Apache, remains a mystery even today. His date of birth, though variously recorded from

1834 to 1845, can be fairly well fixed from several sources at 1838. While the place is a good deal foggier, Louisiana is the leading probability, and Longstreet's heavy Southern "brogue," as it was then called, clearly signaled the general vicinity of his origins. His most distinctive physical feature was the missing ear concealed beneath his long blond hair. It was whispered that when he was only fourteen or fifteen his extraordinary skill with a gun and his precocious fondness for whiskey had won him a place with a gang of horse thieves, located by various narrators in Kentucky, Texas, or Colorado. When the rustlers were caught and hanged, Longstreet was spared because he was so young, but his ear was slashed off to teach him a lesson and to brand him as an outlaw wherever he went.

The legend holds that Longstreet first emerged into the region through which he was to range for nearly half a century at El Dorado, on the Nevada side of the Colorado, after a period of running a flatboat on the river. It is a plausible story but not yet confirmed. Soon after its discovery in 1861, when it was still considered a part of Arizona territory, El Dorado became a haven for outlaws and deserters from the army during the Civil War. Here, where the river ran swift and blue, chollas incandescent with blond thorns glistened on the slopes, and the purpled gray mountains of the Arizona badlands tossed and pitched and heaved in the distance like a troubled dream, Longstreet is said to have run a small store near one of the principal mines, which he had neglected to discover because of overindulgence in whiskey. All this is not unlikely, since Longstreet ran a similar enterprise at a later date; it was always his strange fate to overlook the bonanza at his doorstep and instead spend his energy on a poorer and more distant prospect. Yet no trace of his presence in El Dorado appears in the Lincoln County, Nevada, tax records.

In Arizona territory, the Longstreet story at last begins to move from the legendary into the historical. His first Mohave County mining claim, the Julia, filed on January 1,

Longstreet as Arthur Buel drew him in the *Tonopah Daily Sun*, Aug. 13, 1905 (Nevada Historical Society)

1880, was located near Mike Scanlon's stone cabin in the Lost Basin country. Longstreet's presence at the site and his probable acquaintance with Scanlon lend some strength to newspaper reporter Elton Garrett's story that Longstreet had earlier operated a ferry with Scanlon between present Greggs Hideout and South Cove on the Colorado. When the rush began to Gold Basin in the White Hills on the western rim of the sandy Hualapai Valley about twenty miles south of the ferry, Longstreet was no doubt one of the first on the ground. By the time eager prospectors finished staking every foot of quartz in the district, Longstreet had already filed ten claims.

Ambition thrived, branched, and thickened even more extravagantly than the large old Joshua trees that dotted the Hualapai Valley in the midst of that giddy boom. Ranches were sold; mortgages undertaken; money, and still more money, was needed for the mines. The best of these, the Eldorado, would eventually produce $65,000 worth of bullion, a respectable showing but far short of the great expectations with which the White Hills prospectors had gilded their portions of rock and sand. Every prospector "imagined himself a millionaire," in the words of one observer, and demanded an exorbitant price of $40,000 or even $750,000 for his claim. Another visitor reported, "They may have to pack their wood and water for miles, fare hard and sleep cold, but what does a man care for hardship when he has millions within his grasp?" Longstreet was apparently less optimistic than the rest. Instead of holding out for hundreds of thousands, he sold a half interest in one of his best claims, the Southern Pride (believed to have been part of the Golden Rule mine), in the autumn of 1881, six months after he recorded it. Of his remaining claims, the Julia showed the most promise, and Longstreet apparently continued his efforts to develop it through the spring of 1882.

Longstreet's trading and milling activities in White Hills are more obscure than his development of mining claims.

Several saloons had opened in Lost Basin in the spring of 1882 among the tents, covered wagons, crude stone cabins, and even caves in which the prospectors lived. Possibly Longstreet presided at some such establishment as the combined saloon and butcher shop promising customers good liquors, fat beef, and water for laundry and toilet purposes only. He might have supplied feed for his patrons' teams; the advertisements of a similar Mohave County proprietor cautioned teamsters to "keep their brakes on hard" lest their teams bolt at breakneck speed to reach the "succulent bunch grass" packed from the surrounding hills by his "vigorous and efficient force of Wallapai squaws." In a region where Longstreet's tastes for both high-stakes poker and Indian wives were widely shared, it is fairly certain that a convivial group of squaw men often gathered over cards at his table. His place would probably have been a tent saloon similar to the one that he ran some years later at Sylvania.

Since Longstreet undertook no milling in subsequent years, his later life provides no clues to the type of enterprise he might have run in White Hills. He has not been mentioned in connection with the Grass Springs mill; he may therefore have operated the *arrastra* that the miners installed at Cold Springs, a locale with which his name has been connected. An *arrastra* provided a primitive and tedious method of crushing ore with abrasive stones dragged by a mule plodding in endless circles around a rock-lined pit. Rudimentary as it was, the Cold Springs *arrastra* enabled the Gold Basin miners to earn a little money, instead of seeing all their returns siphoned away in milling and transportation costs.

Minding the slow, wearisome turns of an *arrastra*, however, was an occupation unlikely to please the restless Longstreet for long. He may also have arrived at the conclusion that there were no new Eldorados to be found in the district, as did many of the other prospectors. The once jubilant horde in White Hills began dwindling down to a few stubborn diehards. Gold Basin was unmistakably in eclipse by the autumn of 1883, and prospectors who had refused high prices in the heady days of promise grew desperate for buyers. Longstreet did not remain to see the last of their hopes trickle away in the sands of the Hualapai. With his Indian woman and his notched .44, he had moved on long since.

In the late summer of 1882, he crossed the Colorado River into the Moapa Valley and for the first time became a flesh and blood presence more substantial to the searching eye of history than a name in an old leather-bound book of mining records. He was then forty-four years old, if he spoke true to the voter registration officials of his later years, but he was far from ready for a peaceful decline into old age. More than half his life—and by no means an uneventful half—still lay ahead of him. News of his arrival soon traveled 100 miles north to Pioche, the Lincoln County seat. The jocular account on his doings that appeared in the *Pioche Record* suggests that he was accompanied by one of his Indian wives and a full complement of her relatives. "Ther hes bin, an iz goin to be sum mor, changes made at St. Thomas sune. Mr. Jack Long [Longstreet] iz goin to open a salun an drug store at that place. Mrs. J. an darter hes gon on a visit to Utaw, but this grate stopin plac for the publick is kept up by her sun Charles in her abcent. Mr. Coleman tends to the kulenary department, an Miss Pinenuts iz actin housekeper pro. tem. . . ."

Since Charles was referred to as Mrs. J's son, not Longstreet's, it may be surmised that she had children by a previous marriage. So far as can be determined, Longstreet fathered no children of his own, but if a young widow with strong, round arms and the dark burnished skin he had come to prefer in a woman had taken his eye on some sojourn in a Utah Indian camp, he would not have found a batch of children any barrier to their union. In fact, he might have seen the little ones playing with their burned clay dolls at her feet, squealing as they swung on braided yucca ropes, or hobbling crookedly on stilts between the dome-shaped kanees of brush and bark as a greater asset than the usual Indian dowry of tightly woven baskets and bright beads.

The truth was that despite his taciturnity, his fierce blue stare, and the fear that his deadly prowess with guns inspired in other men, Longstreet was extremely fond of children and more than once informally adopted a desert waif into his cabin and his affections. So if Mrs. J brought him children, as well as an unquestioning willingness to ride with him into the remote deserts where few white women cared to live plus the survival skills of an Indian woman used to scooping the succulent tortoise from its shell or baking ground pinon-nut cakes in the ashes of her campfire, Longstreet would have thought she came to his blanket especially well endowed.

The tiny settlement of St. Thomas where Longstreet opened his saloon and drugstore (a combination of enterprises that promised to cure what ailed a man either one way or the other) was situated at the southern end of the Moapa Valley, often called the Muddy Valley in those days, where the Muddy River flows southeast to join the Virgin as it courses down to meet the Colorado. East of the valley's rich farmland lay the long, level line of Mormon Mesa, straight, ordered, and regular as the Mormon settlers themselves; westward the Muddy range dissolved into the crumpled, red sandstone cliffs of the Valley of Fire.

A substantial colony of Mormons had settled the valley in 1865. Over the next six years they built adobe houses covered with earth or tules, plowed the land, established the towns of St. Thomas, St. Joseph, Overton, and West Point, dug canals, built roads, planted cottonwoods, and began draining the swamps. Then, in 1871, they abruptly departed when government surveyors placed the community within the Nevada state line and the settlers found themselves subject to state taxes four times higher than Utah's.

Despite the church's intensive colonizing efforts, their withdrawal was unlikely to be rebuked. President Brigham

Young had toured the area in 1870 and, far from again remarking that this was the place, told the settler accompany-
ing him, "If the gentiles want that country, they're welcome
to it." The adobe houses started to crumble and wash away;
sand choked the canals; the desert began to move in. Nearly
a decade passed before the tide of settlement began to turn
again. By 1882 a few settlers had homesteaded the best of the
abandoned Mormon lands, a handful of Mormons had returned, and the *Pioche Record's* correspondent on the Muddy
reported a white population of sixty-four in the entire valley.

Not all of them were settlers of an entirely desirable kind. It
was widely acknowledged that a "swarm of murderers and
law breakers" had infested Lincoln County and adjacent
areas in Utah for years. The *Pioche Record* suggested calling
the country near the state border "Murderer's Paradise" because so many eluded pursuit by slipping back and forth
across the boundary line. Disturbing stories of horse thievery and worse filtered north to the county sheriff in Pioche
from time to time. A young stranger driving six mules had
"made a reckless display of a pocket-book well filled with
greenbacks" amounting to several hundred dollars as he
passed through the Moapa Valley. At a point near Coyote
Holes, the young stranger suddenly disappeared, but the
ending to his story could be clearly read in the earth, where
the tracks of his mules had been nearly obliterated by the
hoofprints of many horses descending a desert trail and cutting into the main road. "It is a well known fact that a gang
of desperadoes infest the lower country," observed the *Pioche
Record.*

Apart from the sixty-four white settlers, both Mormons
and desperadoes, the greater part of the area's population
was Southern Paiute (Nuwuvi). Indians had cultivated the
valley long before the arrival of the white men, and a handful
of Indians cultivated it still on the Moapa Reservation, once
envisaged as a major center for Indian resettlement. In 1873,
after the Mormon exodus and less than a decade before

Longstreet's arrival, the U.S. government had dispatched special commissioners John Wesley Powell and G. W. Ingalls to investigate the condition of the Indians and persuade them to enter reservations.

The commissioners reported that the Indians were eager to cultivate the land and raise cattle in the grasslands of the upper valley. The Mormons had already demonstrated the agricultural promise of the area to anyone's satisfaction. Moreover, the tribes living elsewhere expressed themselves ready to move to Moapa, and the 400 Indians already there told Powell that they were willing to live together with the other bands. Commissioner Ingalls advanced a strong argument for the Moapa Reservation as the future residence of more than 2,300 Indians from Nevada and adjacent areas of Utah, Arizona, and California, nearly a quarter of the Indian population of the Great Basin.

In the commissioners' view, not only would the proposed move into an expanded reservation allay settlers' fears of an imminent Indian rising, but also it seemed to offer the best hope for improving the lot of the Indians. During these troubled years, their existence in a nether region between the old and the new worlds was a precarious one. The white men had preempted the best lands, where they had raised their vegetables and hunted, and the game had disappeared. A few learned a little English and found occasional jobs as seasonal laborers for the settlers. Some lived by begging or stealing. Many still struggled to eke out a miserable subsistence on their diminished lands in the old way, living on roots, nuts, berries, seeds, rabbits, rodents, snakes, lizards, grasshoppers, and the like. Others hid in the mountains.

The harshness of their lives was sharpened by the contempt of white men, some of whom regarded them as subhuman. The West's famous historan Hubert Howe Bancroft wrote of the "Diggers," a term applied to both the Shoshones and Paiutes, "having no clothes, scarcely any cooked food, in many instances no weapons, with merely a few vague imaginings for religion, living in the utmost squalor and filth, putting no bridle on their passions, there is surely room for no missing link between them and the brutes."

In the year when Longstreet arrived, the Southern Paiutes of the Moapa must still have looked much as they did when the Ingalls party photographed them in 1873. They lived in kanees like round igloos made of reeds, or sometimes in rough brush shelters. Here they still mashed mesquite beans on their grinding stones, carried water on their backs in big basket jugs, and gathered seeds in baskets. Here they sat before their kanees in the traditional Paiute posture, one knee raised, the other crooked flat on the ground, weaving their baskets and chipping arrowheads to be shot from their four-foot bows. Their faces were dark and gleaming, their black hair straight and smooth, and their bare feet powdered white with dust. The round-armed, strong-handed women were naked to the waist and wore long pieces of cloth, crudely tied around their waists, as skirts; in time they would learn to assume long-sleeved, fringed, loose-fitting clothes. The men wore breechclothes, and sometimes caps, decorated with the curving horns of mountain sheep.

The dark, beetle-browed faces were hard to read. They ranged from the self-conscious pride and disgust of a young scout to the worried expressions of the women. No one smiled, at least not before the intruder with the camera. Sarah Winnemucca, daughter of a northern Paiute chief, has written that all laughter and joy were hidden behind the blank, cowed faces the Indians turned to the white men; they only dared to reveal emotion among themselves because they feared the white destroyer would somehow root out any sign of happiness at the source.

Commissioners Powell and Ingalls had believed the Moapa Reservation lands "good and sufficient" to provide the Indians with a better life. A decade after their report, however, it was evident that two obstacles prevented the Southern Paiutes from successfully farming the valley. The first was

Longstreet often participated in Southern Paiute gambling sessions like this one, photographed near Las Vegas in 1873 (Henry E. Huntington Library)

the perfidy of Colonel W. R. Bradfute, superintending farmer at the Moapa Reservation and ruler of an isolated domain far outside the effective supervision of his superiors. The second was the tenacity of the white settlers, who had not only snatched the best lands but also controlled most of the water rights. The Indians lacked enough water even to plant a crop without the settlers' indulgence, and the government had failed to act on the commissioners' urging that $32,000—a paltry sum in comparison to the military expenses of hostilities with the Indians—should be expended to buy out the settlers. "There is now no great uninhabited and unknown region to which the Indian can be sent," the commissioners had warned. "He is among us, and we must either protect him or destroy him."

Protection was not to be the choice. Not only did the Powell-Ingalls recommendation fail to win government approval, but also the capacity of the Moapa Reservation to provide even for the local Indians appeared increasingly doubtful when the land area set aside for the reservation was sharply reduced by the government in 1875. Increasingly, Indians fled the reservation. But the end came slowly as death to a trapped beast, flailing weakly in the quicksands around the Virgin. While more white men moved steadily into the valley, the remaining Indians at the reservation struggled to farm with the limited water that the settlers deigned to dispense to them, watched the ranchers' stock break into their fields, and read unhappy portents in the strange sunsets that appeared during the winter of 1883–1884.

They beheld the western skies illuminated with flaming red at evening and watched the moon turn a bright golden yellow as the darkness burned scarlet again at dawn. Knowing nothing of the ash spewing into the atmosphere from the distant volcanoes that scientists believed were the cause of this brilliance in the sky, the wise ones read its message to the rest of the tribe, and the proof of their words was everywhere, in the empty kanees of decimated families, the fences that marked their old lands out of bounds, the scarcity of game. As they gazed upon the burning skies above the mountains, they saw the funeral pyre of the Indian people.

By rights Longstreet's new drugstore in St. Thomas should have done a thriving business because, during the period when he opened his shop, fully two-thirds of the valley's settlers were reported laid up with the fever, soon to be followed by measles and the epizootic. The malady had struck just when it was time for the fall plowing for barley and wheat. No doubt he dispensed such popular, all-purpose remedies of the period as Dr. Rush's Blood Root Oil, which promised to cure rheumatism, lumbago, backache, gout, quinsy, sore throat, swellings, sprains, burns, general bodily pains, toothache, earache, headache, frosted feet and ears, and "all other pains and aches."

It appears, however, that the saloon side of Longstreet's enterprise did an even brisker business. "U understan now Sant Tomas is not a town uv the past any longer," declared the *Pioche Record's* Moapa correspondent. "No, sur, she kumin to the frunt, she iz. Mr. Jack Longstreet flung his dores open to the publik on the 17th of Sept., and we've had more fites since than enybody's town—its the salun and drug store I speak uv." Some of these fights may have been disputes related to losses at cards. Another dispatch revealed that Longstreet had "succeeded in 'bagging' all the grain in the valley while instructing the honest ranchers in the various combinations of draw poker."

The riotous pleasures of saloon-keeping in St. Thomas, as well as the more subdued ones of ministering to the sickly in place of a doctor, evidently failed to provide Longstreet with sufficient occupation. Presently he gave up the saloon to homestead 120 acres of land about six miles south of the Moapa Reservation. After a ranch purchased from an Indian was added to the homestead in late January 1883, rumors of unrest among the Indians drifted back to Pioche. Colonel W. R. Bradfute, the official in charge of the Moapa Reservation, wrote that the sale of the ranch had aroused dissatisfaction among the Indians, but subsequent events would show that his explanations of the sources of Indian discontent were not invariably to be believed. The initial assumption in Pioche was that the disturbance had started when horses belonging to rancher Alexander Dry destroyed the Indians' crops—apparently a common occurrence; this may have pressed closer to the truth.

Nonetheless, the mention of Longstreet in connection with the unrest was the first hint that he was becoming a mediator willing to champion Indian interests in the white world. Unlike most white men in the region, Longstreet had listened and learned until he spoke the tongue of the Nuwuvi like a son of the people. He shared their gambling habits and their cactus wine, he came to see the beauty in the winged black brows and ripe bodies of their women, and finally he found it impossible to ignore their grievances. In time, Longstreet's attempts to right the wrongs of his adopted people would bring a full measure of trouble down upon his head. But several years were still to pass before his protest came into the open. In the interim, the Indians retreated steadily from the valley toward the reservation and the mountains beyond, the returning Mormons continued to siphon up Moapa land, purchasing those properties that could not be homesteaded, and the mysterious trouble subsided—for the time being.

The fourth phenomenon to accompany Jack Longstreet's appearance in the Moapa Valley—alongside saloon fighting, draw poker, and Indian unrest—was an impassioned spate of horse racing. Almost until the day he died Longstreet harbored a taste for fine horses and a keen interest in racing, to which the pioneer settlers responded with gusto. Much time was spent in careful, narrow-eyed appraisal of the horses, in smoothing and marking the track, in gathering the purse. Tent saloons were set up for the occasion, if none of the permanent variety was at hand, and watermelons and pumpkins were devoured in the summer season. Prospectors rode down out of the hills with gold slugs or gold dust in their pockets to bet; a sixty-mile ride was nothing, if a race lay at the end of it. Hundreds of dollars, even thousands, sometimes all that a man possessed—horses, oxen, wagons, land—might be bet on these races. Desperate "plungers" had even been known to strip off their clothes and throw them on the betting pile. And sometimes it all ended in fisticuffs, even homicide.

Such passions were plainly gathering in St. Thomas on the Saturday in late February when Longstreet raced his Indian pony against Pat Curlin's horse. In the warm climate of the Moapa Valley, spring comes early. The alfalfa fields were already greening, the grain silky with young shoots, and the cottonwoods "beginning to breathe" in the balmy sunshine. Curlin had just sold his ranch to the Mormons for $1,500 and

A Nevada race like those in which a Longstreet horse often pounded to victory. This contest was held at the Tonopah railroad day celebration in 1904 (Jim Wolfe Collection, Central Nevada Historical Society)

"went to horse racing." He spent $120 on a fine horse he believed could beat anything on four feet and hired a trainer to exercise the animal until it reached the peak of its form. He then bet $1,205, nearly the entire purchase price of his ranch, that his new horse would beat Longstreet's Indian pony. (Were a man to wager the greater part of the purchase price of his ranch on a single race today, the amount would range from several hundred thousand to several million dollars.) Somehow, no doubt with considerable help from his friends, Longstreet managed to match the bet, an unusually large one for a Lincoln County race in that period. Then, either through his own foolishness or Longstreet's connivance,

Curlin's jockey incapacitated himself just before the great event. In the jocular words of the *Pioche Record*: "Pat was depending mainly upon his rider, but the night before the Chief of the Muddy Islands was doped, and his drawers, night-cap and night-shirt stolen. James Oles, who was trainer, under the circumstances, consented to ride." When the two horses thundered down the 440–yard track, Longstreet's Indian pony streaked ahead. "Pat is short $1,205 somewhere," the press reported, "besides a good horse and a small bill of expenses."

Perhaps Longstreet's financial condition steadily improved on the fleet heels of the Indian pony, or perhaps Pat Curlin's lost fortune made the rounds among Moapa's aficionados of the turf, as it was repeatedly won and lost. About a year later Longstreet won a $1,000 purse from another rancher and promptly lost it on the next race to Alexander Dry, owner of a large spread near the Moapa Reservation and much stock, including a great herd of horses.

Despite rumors that Dry had forcibly commandeered a horse from Longstreet, this lost race became the accepted explanation of what began to be cryptically known in Lincoln County as "a difficulty about a horse" between the two ranchers. Yet it is also possible that their quarrel had started much earlier when Dry's horses trampled and devoured the Indian crops. Longstreet probably took the Indians' part.

As spring warmed toward summer, the breach between them appeared to have healed. They encountered each other in St. Thomas on a Saturday in May, possibly tilted a glass or two in an amicable way, and rode north together "apparently friends." Appearances were entirely at odds with the reality. On the part of at least one of them, and possibly both, the outward good fellowship concealed a darker purpose.

Longstreet presently returned to St. Thomas to declare that he had shot Alexander Dry. As he told it, Dry had suddenly covered him with his gun when the two of them reached the sandy banks at the big bend of the Muddy River, and he had been "forced into killing Dry" to protect his own life. Unless he lied, Dry's aim must have been poor, or Longstreet may have saved himself by dropping swiftly down behind his horse, as he was prone to do in such emergencies.

In any case there were no witnesses to contradict him. St. Thomas's justice of the peace, James Ross Megarrigle, an old Scotsman who had once taught school at the Moapa Reservation, believed his story, and Longstreet was promptly set free. This was by no means exceptional on the Nevada frontier, where exoneration by a coroner's jury on grounds of justifiable homicide was the usual aftermath of a fatal affray. Nonetheless, the penchant of the *Pioche Record* to find poetic justice in Dry's death suggests a shade of sensitivity over the ease with which the law had accepted Longstreet's version of events. The *Record* pointed out that in the autumn of 1878 Dry had killed John Hanly, foreman at the Kearney ranch adjoining his own, and he too had gone free, there being no witnesses to gainsay him. Further irony might have been perceived in the circumstance that Hanly had also been killed in a row following a horse race.

Dry, one of only two bachelors in the valley, left no obvious heir, nor had he made a will, not having figured on dying so soon. Consequently, his large herds of horses and cattle went up for auction by the county. To this end, the public administrator, designated simply as "Billy" in the press, and his assistants journeyed down to the Moapa to drive Dry's stock north to Pioche. The Moapa settlers thought the simple expedient of holding the auction at Moapa would have brought less hardship to the stock and less expense to the taxpayers.

When the *Pioche Record*'s Moapa correspondent signing himself "Blow Fly" wrote a series of coarse burlesque on the "caravan of so-called cowboys," he undoubtedly elicited a good many guffaws around the Muddy. Blow Fly accused the public administrator of caching his grub in order to transport candies, perfumery, and a wide variety of other entrancing presents to the girls of St. Thomas. "The girls are de-

lighted with the sundowns [broad-brimmed hats] and say
they are 'just splendid to gather chips in,' and 'the palpitators
hatch turkey eggs to perfection.' Billy has arranged the business with a muscle." Blow Fly then depicted the "young
army" fighting among themselves over the molasses jug on
the return journey and lobbing mudballs at Billy as he sat
unhappily on his wagon, mired in the middle of the stream.
Few could disagree with Blow Fly's conclusion:

> It is predicted that after the estate is finished being admin-
> istered upon, it will be very dry indeed, in the fullest sense
> of the word. It is a shame and an outrage. When the Omni-
> potent summons me up to the Golden Throne, I will take
> good care to leave no estate to be administered upon, not
> even an old bursted patent bustle.

Two more summers would pass before Longstreet's name
again appeared in the news. Those summers in the Moapa
were an ordeal that only the hardy could endure. An egg in
the sand roasted in quick time. Chickens began to raise their
wings and gasp for breath at dawn. Barefoot schoolgirls
scampered home a few steps at a time, throwing their aprons
on the ground to stand on as they went. Settlers rolled in the
ditches to cool off. At night they abandoned their stifling
adobes to sleep on the roofs of the sheds, pestered by hordes
of mosquitoes but secure in the knowledge that they were
temporarily beyond the reach of the scorpions, tarantulas,
and rattlesnakes.

It was during these dog days of July 1886 that the *Pioche
Record* reported the appearance in the settlements of Utah
and Lincoln County of an eloquent and charming gentleman
in a blue suit and cork hat by the name of La Belle. He represented himself as a former jockey, now in delicate health,
and the representative of a San Francisco sewing machine
company. He sojourned in Pioche, he spent time in Bullionville and Panaca, he hired horses as he traveled in a leisurely
way to the other little settlements of the region to repair sew-

ing machines; and everywhere he went he delighted crowds of people with his many entertaining stories of Mexico, the "southern country at large," and especially Arizona.

We can only speculate on whether some of these stories may have touched upon the shadowy past of the big, crop-eared rancher in the Moapa Valley. It is just possible that Longstreet and La Belle had known each other in El Dorado Canyon or in Arizona, perhaps in connection with the races in which La Belle had ridden, and that there was already bad blood between them. If not, there soon would be.

John Hartey, a resident of Bullionville, abruptly decided that the horse obtained from him by the charming and gentlemanly Mr. La Belle had not been hired but stolen. Thievery was a matter with which Hartey was thoroughly conversant, as became clear some years later when he, his family, and his friends were arrested for relieving a traveling peddler who had unwisely stopped for the night at the Hartey ranch of several hundred dollars' worth of goods. In 1886, however, he had not yet been exposed as the fox in the chicken coop. When Hartey, in his role as the upright citizen victimized by a scoundrel, rode out after La Belle, he was accompanied by Jack Longstreet.

The mystery that followed was never satisfactorily resolved. Hartey had telegraphed to Mineral Park, Arizona, that La Belle should be arrested because he was a fugitive from justice with a stolen horse. La Belle made a hasty exit from Arizona before that could occur, writing Hartey from St. Thomas that he would return the horse. He nonetheless made no apparent effort to do so but instead abruptly departed for Milford, Utah, a move that much resembled the familiar practice of border hopping that enabled many a guilty man to elude the law. Hartey then persuaded law officers to deputize him and set off with Longstreet on a ride of nearly 200 miles to arrest La Belle at Milford. In an age when the victims of minor horse thievery were often advised by the press to redress their wrongs by stealing one back from the next thief they encountered, it seems a very long way to go over just one horse.

After arresting La Belle, Hartey and Longstreet turned back, apparently herding their prisoner in front of the wagon on the pretext that the exercise would keep him warm in the cold November air. At a point near Desert Springs, something suddenly spooked the team. The horses bucked wildly, then balked. While Longstreet and Hartey struggled to control them, La Belle fled to a little clump of junipers. By the time Longstreet and Hartey were able to follow, he had unaccountably disappeared. In a desert so barren that no sagebrush grew tall enough to hide a rabbit, it seemed that the ground had opened and swallowed him—at least, so said Longstreet and Hartey. Some days later the Shoal Creek postmaster found La Belle's frozen body lying near the road.

He was declared to have died of exposure, a verdict in which the Utah sheriff concurred. However, some who had seen La Belle's body claimed that it contained three bullet holes and the sheriff was simply reluctant to pursue the matter. The investigation promised by Utah authorities evidently vanished with the same alacrity attributed to La Belle himself at Desert Springs. But a question remained, squarely posed by the *Pioche Record*: "Was there a bullet hole through the brain of the unfortunate, or was there not? We seek the truth—we have been informed both ways."

Notes

Longstreet's early life is briefly discussed in his obituary in the *Tonopah* (Nevada) *Mining Record*, July 28, 1928; Carl B. Glasscock, *Gold in Them Hills* (New York: Grosset & Dunlap, 1932), 212–13; and William Caruthers, *Loafing Along Death Valley Trails* (Pomona, Calif.: P-B Press, 1951), 90.

Longstreet's activities in El Dorado Canyon and northern Arizona are mentioned in his obituary and in Elton Garrett, "Nuggets of Boulder Color," *Las Vegas Review-Journal*, February 23, 1933. Possibly the reference to the White Hills mine in El Dorado Canyon is a garbled allusion to the Eldorado mine in White Hills, Arizona, an area where Longstreet's presence can be confirmed. On El Dorado Canyon, see John L. Riggs, "The Reign of Violence in El Dorado Canyon," *Third Biennial Report of the Nevada Historical Society, 1911-1912* (Carson City: State Printing Office, 1913), 95-107; John M. Townley, "El Dorado Canyon and Searchlight Mining Districts," *Nevada Historical Society Quarterly* 11 (Spring 1968): 5-19; and Myron Angel, ed., *History of Nevada* (Oakland, Calif.: Thompson & West, 1881), 484, 489-90.

The major source on Gold Basin is Robert Lenon, "The Mines of Gold Basin: A Report of 1883," *Journal of Arizona History* 8 (1967): 256-68. Items on Gold Basin-Lost Basin appear in *Alta Arizona* from November 1881 through May 1882; the issues of November 12, 1881, and March 18, 1882, are especially pertinent. Longstreet's prospecting in the region from January 1, 1880, to April 19, 1882, can be traced in the Index to Mining Claims in the Mohave County courthouse, Kingman, Arizona. Early Mohave County mining is reviewed in Richard J. Hinton, *The Handbook to Arizona: Its Resources, History, Towns, Mines, Ruins, and Scenery* (Glorieta, N. Mex.: Rio Grande Press, 1878), 76, 159-67.

The following works on the Indians were consulted: *Nuwuvi: A Southern Paiute History* (Reno: Inter-Tribal Council of Nevada, 1976), especially 92-108; G. W. Ingalls, "Indians of Nevada," in Sam P. Davis, ed., *History of Nevada*, vol. I (Reno and Los Angeles: Elms Publishing, 1913), 20-189; Don D. Fowler and Catherine S. Fowler, eds., *Anthropology of the Numa: John Wesley Powell's Manuscripts on the Numic Peoples of Western North America, 1868-1880* (Washington, D.C.: Smithsonian Institution Press, 1971); Sarah Winnemucca Hopkins, *Life Among the Piutes: Their Wrongs and Claims* (Bishop, Calif.: Sierra Media, 1969, originally published in 1883); and Virginia C. Trenholm and Maurine Carley, *The Shoshonis: Sentinels to the Rockies* (Norman: University of Oklahoma Press, 1964).

Many valuable details on the Moapa Valley appear in Pearson S. Corbett, "Settling the Muddy River Valley," *Nevada Historical Society Quarterly* 18 (Fall 1975): 141-51; and Arabell L. Hafner, ed., *One Hundred Years on the Muddy* (Springville, Utah: Art City Publishing, 1967). Longstreet's arrival was reported in the *Pioche Record*, Sept. 16 and Oct. 14, 1882. On the Curlin-Longstreet horse race, see the *Pioche Record,* March 3, 1883. Other races in Lincoln County and other locales are covered in the issues of August 19, September 9, and October 14, 1882, and the *Carson City Daily Appeal,* June 5, 1907.

Alexander Dry's story appears in the May 17, August 16, August 23, August 30, September 6, and September 13, 1884, issues of the *Pioche Record,* the May 21, 1884, issue of the Austin *Daily Reveille,* and Angel, *History of Nevada,* 355. Mining camp homicide is discussed in Roger D. McGrath, *Gunfighters, Highwaymen, & Vigilantes: Violence on the Frontier* (Berkeley and Los Angeles: University of California Press, 1984), especially pp. 84–85.

For the La Belle affair, see the *Pioche Weekly Record,* November 20, November 27, December 4, December 11, and December 25, 1886. Hartey's arrest was reported in the *Belmont Courier,* March 3, 1900.

2

Moapa Reservation

While there were some happy and honest exceptions to the rule, venality among Indian agents and the farmer-agents placed in charge of the smaller reservations continued to plague the Bureau of Indian Affairs throughout the 1880s. At one reservation after another it was the same sorry story: phantom sawmills, grist mills, and other buildings never built for the Indians, while government appropriations for their construction mysteriously disappeared; clothing and blankets sold for profit instead of being distributed to the Indians for whom they were intended; rental charges for the farming tools, seeds, and draft animals that the agents were supposed to provide to the Indians free of charge; the exaction by agents of such large proportions of reservation produce that the Indian farmers effectively became sharecroppers; the rental of the best Indian lands to white settlers as an extra perquisite for the agent; rental fees levied upon the Indians for using their own land. Sarah Winnemucca observed that the Indian agents "get rich very soon, so that they can have their gold-headed canes, with their names engraved on them." Colonel Bradfute did not, so far as is known, go in for gold-headed canes, but Longstreet soon discovered how he treated the Indians. No doubt it was this that lay at the root of the escalating quarrel between the two men.

To most settlers in the Moapa, Bradfute's treatment of the Indians was a matter of indifference. They disliked him for other reasons. The *Pioche Record* might favorably describe him as "kindly" Colonel Bradfute, the "boss granger" of the Moapa, but his neighbors found him a foul-tempered, drunken, Simon Legree of the desert, living like a recluse in niggardly squalor while he amassed more wealth through sharp dealings with the Indians. The agricultural acumen of the boss granger was also open to question, as on the occasion when Bradfute planted and carefully tended an apple orchard, only to discover at harvest time that his rows of young trees were really quaking aspens. It may be noted that, as reservation farmer, instructing the Indians in agricultural matters was among his primary duties.

In a cabin not far from his father lived Bradfute's son, John Jr., well known for an addiction to the jug that rivaled that of his venerable parent. A humorous story went the rounds in the Moapa about a traveling missionary who stopped by John Jr.'s cabin. When the young divine declined to partake of the jug, John convinced him that the region was crawling with rattlesnakes, and that frequent and liberal libations were the only means by which a man could immunize his system against snakebite. The young missionary eventually embarked on a howling drunk. Some in the Moapa had been heard to suggest that if the jug possessed even a small part of the medicinal properties young John attributed to it, both he and his father could stroll through a nest of coiled and buzzing diamondbacks with impunity.

It was in the course of passing the jug during a "convivial entertainment" at Phil Wright's hostelry on the Moapa that the long-simmering hostility between Colonel Bradfute and Longstreet at last broke into the open. Bradfute had emerged from his customary seclusion one day in mid-May 1887, at the time of year when people joked that the mosquitoes floating over the sagebrush attain the size of sandhill cranes, and encountered Longstreet. After both repaired to Wright's for refreshments, in company with several other men, an altercation ensued, later recounted in the *Pioche Record*:

The generous wine of mine host warmed up the stomachs of the guests and the fumes of the spirit eventually percolated their brains and incited the awakening of trivial animosities, which had slept for many months in the breasts of Bradfute and Longstreet, each of whom had kept locked up within his heart, with all the stoicism of the Indian, a $5 poker debt and a $2 beef bill to offset it. In the midst of the hilarity which ensued, a gentleman whose appellation is Black Jack, became a topic of conversation [probably the outlaw "Black Jack" Kellett, who may have purchased quarter interests in Longstreet's Julia and Mono mines in Lost Basin and who had allegedly worsted Longstreet in a St. Thomas fistfight] and it would seem that Jack's reputation was quite freely discussed by the Colonel, as was also the reputation of Longstreet, both of which the Colonel pronounced as being decidedly bad. Then Bradfute dropped his right hand to his side, upon which Mr. Longstreet (with the view that the Colonel was on the point of bombarding him with a masked battery, which Longstreet supposed the Colonel to carry,) snaked out his own battery with one hand and with the other hit the Colonel a diff alongside the jaw, knocking the old man off the box on which he was sitting to the ground. Afterward, on the outside of the house, Longstreet hit the Colonel another clip, which wound up hostilities for the time being.

Determined to vent his rancor against Longstreet even if it took a hundred-mile ride, the angry colonel set off to Pioche, where he swore out a warrant for assault and battery against Longstreet. Sheriff Turner and his deputy journeyed south to arrest Longstreet, and it appears that a certain friendliness developed between the law officers and their tall, long-haired prisoner during the lengthy trek back to Pioche. On May 31, 1887, Longstreet stood trial and was promptly acquitted.

Pioche was obviously incensed over this "farce of a trial" at the taxpayers' expense, "all on account of a black eye induced by bug juice." Recourse to the law for anything short of murder was considered decidedly panty-waisted, a sentiment that the verdict may have been intended to convey to Bradfute. The colonel himself ascribed his failure to secure redress from the law to another cause, one rather reminiscent of the circumstances surrounding the sudden retirement of Pat Curlin's jockey. Bradfute claimed that the sheriff and a wealthy rancher who was friendly with Longstreet had fixed the jury and after additional fulminations went on to say that the presiding justice was "so drunk he could not hold his head up." The judge and jurors were "taken to the saloon and filled full of whiskey before the court was opened. I am sixty-four years old but I never witnessed such degredation in a court of Justice before."

Now it was Longstreet's turn for revenge, and it appears that he may have told Bradfute of his intention to expose Bradfute's reprehensible treatment of the Indians to government authorities. Unwittingly, Longstreet was moving into the role that historians have found was typically played by squaw men at the Indian agencies throughout the West during the frontier period—defender of Indian interests in the white world.

Why Longstreet, who was accustomed to settling differences with his shooting iron, should have chosen to denounce Bradfute by writing to his superiors is by no means clear. Perhaps a shootout with a man as elderly as Bradfute seemed less than sporting. Perhaps he was aware that Bradfute was urging government authorities to prosecute him as a cattle thief, and figured, as a Southern duelist would, that the choice of weapons had been Bradfute's.

Or maybe Longstreet had lived so long with the Indians

that he had come to see death as they did. Life was precarious; death, frequent and swift, and when it came, it meant no more than a short, light step from sunlight into shadow. As the Cheyenne say, "Only stones stay on earth forever." Thinking thus, he may have meant to part Bradfute from the profits that seemed the sole purpose of his existence and to punish him with something worse than a bullet—disgrace. No one knew the meaning of disgrace better than a man who bore his scar like a brand everywhere he went.

Longstreet was, so far as we know, the only man in the Moapa to speak out against the injustices suffered by the Indians under Bradfute, and four years later in Sylvania would again be seen trying to bring crude redress against another oppressive figure. So perhaps it was something more than spite toward Bradfute or the need to defend himself against his adversary's charges that pricked him three weeks later in the Moapa Valley. He could easily have melted away into the countryside as he knew so well how to do. But instead he remained obstinately at home on his ranch, risking much—if he was indeed a wanted man. As he laid out the ruled paper and awkwardly gripped the unfamiliar pen in his big hand, he may have been moved by grievances a good deal larger than his own.

The resulting documents, one written on June 20 to Nevada Indian agent W. D. Gibson at his headquarters at the Pyramid Lake reservation, and the other on June 26 to the Secretary of the Interior, are the only writings by Longstreet that have as yet been uncovered. Their grammar and spelling suggest an early encounter with some frontier school but not too prolonged an acquaintance. The second of these letters (the two were nearly identical) informed the secretary:

Sir   I Charge Mr. W. R. Bradfute of the Moapa Reservation or the Mudy River agency of being corrupt dishonest and incompetent to preform the duties of farmer at this agency.

Specifications

1.   I charge him with killing and selling Goverment catell for his own use and benifit

2.   I charge him with hiring out those Goverment mules
for pay and converting the same to his own use and benifit

3.   I charge him with hiring men to brand the anuel increas of the Goverment catell and paying for the same with
Goverment property

4.   I charge him with willfull neglect to look after the
Goverment property comited to his charge Resulting in a
totell loos to the Goverment of more than 500 head of catell
since he took charge here there have been branded something over 300 calves whitch togather with there increas
can not be acounted for

5.   he has Rented out the Goverment land to private
parties that raised their on severall hundered bushells of
Grain using the Goverments farming impliments and the
Goverments team and taking in payment there for a part
of the crop whitch he sold and coverted to his own use and
benifit

finaly

I charge him with conducting the agency soley for his
own pecuniary benifit and with a totell disregard to the
wellfair of the indians

I their fore demand an investigation when I shall be pre-
pard to prove all of the above charges

Bradfute, evidently aware that these charges were forth-
coming, had already endeavored to deflect them by a letter to
his superior, Agent Gibson, on June 11. Following some re-
marks on the continued destruction of the Indian crops by
roving cattle from the government herd, in which he displayed a new and tender concern for the Indians, Bradfute
went on to suggest that Longstreet had been engaged in the
thievery of horses and reservation cattle. However, he can-
didly noted that prosecuting Longstreet on this charge would

not be an easy matter, largely because of the necessity to bribe witnesses who would otherwise be unwilling to testify on his behalf:

> In reference to A. J. Longstreet I am fearful that a case cannot be sustained against him . . as all the Indians upon whom I am depending as witnesses are participants with him in the crime . . this is the opinion of the district attorney of this county, unless I can find out throgh an interpreter others who were not mixed up with them . . there is no one here now that can interpret sufficiently to find them out . . and I am wholy unable to speak the language. . . . My previous statements are true but this version of the case makes me very doubtful as to the final results, then the Indians would have to be satisfied or made so before they are taken to Carson that they would not be molested or abused in any way. & then they will do nothing without they are paid for it, which would be another point in law against us should the opposing attourney discover it upon the whole it is a very notty case to handle. . . .

Bradfute concluded: "A failure to convict would make matters worse. Longstreet is [a] bad man and capable of any crime that is known."

Agent Gibson, having read these charges and countercharges, aligned himself with Bradfute and sent Bradfute's letter, together with his own commentary, to J. D. C. Atkins, Commissioner of Indian Affairs in Washington, D.C. While acknowledging that he was unfamiliar with the Moapa Reservation, having visited it just once for a few hours' time, Gibson explained that he believed Bradfute, primarily because no accusations of dishonesty had previously been lodged against him. Gibson also argued that a small increase in the size of the reservation cattle herd demonstrated that Longstreet's charges concerning Bradfute's machinations with the cattle were "flimsy." He thought "Longstreet may have done this to screen himself or to gratify a revengeful feeling." Wide experience had shown Gibson that "criminals when removed or detected, are ready to cry out 'wolf.' " He did not, however, recommend prosecution of Longstreet, and his high estimate of $1,000 to $3,000 in trial expenses suggests that prosecution was an undertaking he was by no means anxious to pursue.

The matter was presently referred to the acting Commissioner of Indian Affairs. Although he requested that the U.S. Attorney prosecute Longstreet, legal action did not ensue, no doubt because government lawyers found the evidence insufficient and recognized that Bradfute was rapidly backing away from his initial charges. On July 13 the Acting Commissioner wrote his conclusion to the Secretary, "I consider Longstreet unworthy of belief." The sole foundation cited for this opinion, aside from the Gibson and Bradfute letters, was the word of a Washington visitor of the previous year who had praised the reservation farmer.

Commissioner Atkins and the acting Secretary of the Interior were less convinced. Bradfute was scarcely a disinterested party, the caller was probably a friend of his, and officeholders and their advocates were well known in Washington. It was abundantly clear that Agent Gibson neither knew anything about conditions at the Moapa nor acknowledged any responsibility for finding out. Even if he had belatedly done so, he was by now compromised by his own laxity. Moreover, the weight of probability rested on Longstreet's side: charges of corruption in the Indian service had often proved all too well founded. Also, officials may have been perceived something in Longstreet's unlettered scrawl concerning the "wellfair of the indians" that sounded like the sharp ring of truth.

Accordingly, toward the end of September, the acting secretary wrote a note to Commissioner Atkins, and the commissioner decided to dispatch an independent investigator for the dual purpose of closing down the Moapa as a subagency and investigating the charges. The commissioner's instructions revealed two conflicting currents of thought: a presumption that Bradfute was a "man of good judgment" whose advice might be relied upon "with confidence" and an apprehension that the "actual condition of affairs" at the Moapa might prove very different from the representations of Gibson and Bradfute.

The ensuing reports by Special Indian Agent Henry S. Welton of Kingman, Arizona, are the only disinterested evidence we have on the Longstreet-Bradfute dispute. In addition, they bear graphic witness to the remoteness and privation of the Moapa region. After receiving a September 24 letter from the commissioner with instructions to investigate and report on affairs at the reservation, Welton set off on a nine-day march over 230 miles of desert to reach the Moapa. He noted that he started the trek "very *poorly prepared.* taking but one blanket, a shawl, and but little food. but soon found *every one* must take their own supplies as nothing can be bought on the way." Welton was not again to sleep in a bed until his return to civilization.

Welton reported:

On arriving at the reservation I found Mr. Bradfute living like a miserly Hermit. He was without meat coffee or in fact any thing and living on squashes. He has not been out from there in over 8 years (since he went in) I gave him Bacon Sugar Coffee etc   He told me had had no meat in over three monthes and others told me he at one time lived three weeks on *watermelons* alone.

However, Bradfute's eccentric diet concerned Special Agent Welton less than did the situation he found at the reservation. It contained 400 acres of good, arable land, but only 35 were under cultivation. A mere six Indian families lived "camping" on the reservation while Bradfute rented out the cultivated land to white ranchers "for *his own* benefit." (Bradfute's stewardship had apparently contributed to a

sharp decline from the level of 370 acres under cultivation by
a large number of resident Indians in the vicinity of West
Point noted by Ingalls in 1874.) Welton was unable to estimate the current population of the tribe "as they are scaterd
over the surrounding country for 200 miles in all directions."
Welton hoped to persuade twenty to twenty-five families to
reside on the reservation. This would necessitate the promise
of a cow to each family and the far greater incentive of Bradfute's departure, for the Indians "refuse to come while he
remains."

Welton at once set to work to put matters in order on the
reservation. He saw to it that reservation lands were enclosed by fencing or mescrew hedges, and Bradfute's ideas
on where the fence line should be run were acidly rejected ("I
shall surely take *all* the land that belongs to the Indians").
As he endeavored to advertise the sale of the government
herd in preparation for abandoning the Moapa as a subagency, Welton wrote to disabuse his superiors of their mis-
conceptions about the region:

> You speak of having the printing done at *Overton*. Overton
> is 22 miles from the reserve, and contains but three fami-
> lies, all living in Adobe Houses with dirt floors. St. Joe
> (where you speak of advertising) contains but *one* house.
> where a man widower named Logan lives by himself. All
> other "surrounding settlements" are of the same charac-
> ter. *This* [St. George, Utah] is the nearest town, (114 miles)
> and is still 125 miles from a R[ail], Road I wanted my
> printing done here but there is no press

And above all, he attended to the prime necessity—the
dismissal of Bradfute, who unceremoniously departed from
the Moapa without further delay:

> I am sorry to find Mr Bradfute has the ill will not only of all
> his white neighbors, but of the Indians as well. He is 65
> years old, irritable and stuborn, is opposed to giving out

the land in severalty, or leaving the mules harness wagon
[e]tc for their general use and benefit. and as *he* had no
plan to offer or sugestions to make (except for the Govt. to
continue to keep a manager there) and as I could get much
more assistance from both Whites & Indians in his absence, I discontinued his services from the date of my re-
ceipts to agent Gibson. *Manual labor* is all I require, and *he*
is unfited by *age*, disposition, education, and *habits*, for
that.

On December 28 Welton returned from his second journey
to the Moapa and mailed his final report to Washington. Believing that the location of the range made it impossible to
prevent annual thefts of stock from the government herd,
Welton considered that Bradfute's neglectful practices were
not the cause of these losses, nor did he find Bradfute guilty
of butchering and selling government cattle for profit. However, he fully sustained Longstreet's charges that Bradfute
had rented reservation lands, as well as the government
mule team, to private parties, and had in general conducted
the agency solely for his own pecuniary benefit. As evidence
he included an affidavit from George Segmiller, a Moapa Indian living on the reservation:

I know WR Bradfute he had been our Agent many years.
He does not like Indian. . . . He did not let the indians use
team, plow, shovels hoes or other tools. He took away the
bellows because the indians wanted to use the blacksmith
tools. He did not allow indians to use the grindstone without pay. it belonged to the government   we did not pay
him but ground our axes in his absence.

All the same, government authorities decided not to prefer
charges against Bradfute following his dismissal, for Welton
had already urged that he "should be shown some lenity for
having had to live so long in such a place." The Indians were
left to shift for themselves upon their reservation without

further supervision by a resident farmer. Welton expressed the hopeful, if somewhat naive, opinion that they would be able to sustain themselves without encroachment from the cattlemen.

As for Bradfute's accuser, Welton found "the general character and reputation of A. J. Longstreet to be (in the main) as represented by Farmer Bradfute . . . but am unable to obtain any evidence upon which a reasonable probability of his conviction could be based. and as he has now left the State, being last heard from in San Bernardino Co. Cala, I would recommend no further action in his case." Longstreet had indeed made himself scarce. Knowing that Bradfute's conduct of the Moapa Reservation would speak for itself and there would be no need to prove his charges, he was free to concentrate upon his own survival, but it is doubtful that he had found it necessary to withdraw as far as San Bernardino. He might have gone no farther than the Valley of Fire on the western rim of the Moapa, guiding his horse up the narrow defile, past the spot where squiggled petroglyph markings had been scratched through the black desert varnish into the red sandstone beneath, until he reached the small pool in the rock basin. A few years later it would sustain Mouse, the renegade Indian, as it had probably given sanctuary to many a renegade before him.

The country offered many secret places like this one to serve the purpose of a fugitive. One of the affidavits Welton forwarded to his superiors attesting that Bradfute was "habitualy fond of intoxicating drinks and was often drunk" came from E. B. Kiel, notorious for sheltering outlaws at his Las Vegas Valley ranch, and suspected of even worse; it is amusing to reflect that Kiel may have been fully cognizant of Longstreet's whereabouts—perhaps at his own table—at the very time that he gave his testimony to Welton. Or it would have been easy for Longstreet to take refuge high in the smooth, rounded tan cliffs of upper El Dorado Canyon in one of the smoke-blackened caves where some believe the ancient ones had gone to pray. The possibilities were many, and Longstreet had been ranging the country long enough to learn more than a few of them.

Chris Zabriskie, later to become the Death Valley borax king, recalled that on August 4, 1887, Longstreet had saved him by shoeing his team of horses when he was stranded in the desert two hundred miles from a blacksmith. Forty years later Zabriskie wrote Longstreet a grateful letter commemorating that well-remembered day when, in the words of the *Tonopah* (Nevada) *Mining Record*, "a drink of water was worth all the money in the world, and where a nail dropped from the shoe of a horse might spell death for the rider." Zabriskie's letter suggests that, despite the deadly heat of midsummer, Longstreet had veered into the environs of Death Valley during the interval between his denunciation and the resulting investigation of Bradfute.

The exact date of Longstreet's return to the Moapa Valley is uncertain, but it is clear that he had been losing interest in his ranch for some time. Theodore H. Mills, a partially disabled Union veteran who lived in the Meadow Valley Wash, looked after the property in his absence, and Longstreet allowed it to slide onto the delinquent tax list. He had evidently returned by September 1888, when the *Pioche Record* listed him as a precinct judge in Overton; we may be certain that his full political weight was cast on the side of the Democrats, the party with which he had solidly aligned himself like the true Southerner he was.

Candidates in the approaching election obviously believed that his influence was considerable and did not hesitate to remind him of past favors. John C. Kelley dispatched a letter to Longstreet on October 9: "Having shown my willingness to befriend you when you were here on trial for beating Colonel Bradfute, I now appeal to you for assistance at the coming election as I am on the Democratic ticket for the Clerkship." Ed Pierson, Democratic candidate for the state legislature, also wrote to "Friend Jack": "I think I have a very hard fight to make and would be very thankful for all the assistance you can give me—please look around and see how I stand in your precinct." Nonetheless, Longstreet's influence proved insufficient to prevent Pierson's defeat in the statewide Republican landslide of 1888.

By now Longstreet owed the county more than $600 in taxes on the ranch. On September 28 he sold the 240-acre spread of the best land in the valley for $1,200 to Hiram Wiser, whose name it afterward bore on the maps. Within twenty-five years, Longstreet would see its price climb to $50,000. No matter. It had given good graze to the Indian pony for a time, and that was enough. He had not ridden west to increase his herds and irrigate his crops and dicker beside his wagon in the mining towns for the top price. No big white ranch house with a shady veranda amidst a colony of stables and granaries for Jack Longstreet. Instead he turned his broad back on the fields of fertile black land that had once been his, pointing his team past the next wide valley and the dust-colored mesa braceleted with terraces, and headed farther west into wilder country.

Notes

On Indian agents, see Hopkins, *Life Among the Piutes*, especially Chapter 5. The Longstreet-Bradfute controversy is chronicled in a series of letters in the National Archives, Washington, D.C.: W. R. Bradfute to W. D. Gibson, Nevada Indian Agent, June 11, 1887; A. J. Longstreet to Gibson, June 20, 1887, and to Secretary of the Interior, June 26, 1887; Gibson to J. D. C. Atkins, Commissioner of Indian Affairs, June 27, 1887; Acting Commissioner of Indian Affairs to Secretary of the Interior, July 13, 1887; Acting Secretary of the Interior to Commissioner, September 21, 1887; Atkins to Special Indian Agent Henry S. Welton, September 20 and 24, 1887; Acting Commissioner to Welton, October 24, 1887; Welton to Commissioner, November 3, 1887 (with enclosed deposition by W. R. Bradfute dated October 29, 1887); Welton to Commissioner, November 24 and December 28, 1887 (with enclosed depositions by E. B. Kiel, December

8, 1887, and George Segmiller, December 12, 1887). Additional material on Longstreet's trial for assault appears in the *Pioche Record*, June 4, 1887. On the Zabriskie letter, see the *Tonopah* (Nevada) *Mining Record*, August 6, 1927.

Longstreet's alleged fistfight with "Black Jack" Kellett is recounted in Georgia Lewis, "Jack Longstreet," *The Nevadan* (May 18, 1969), 4. Purchases from Longstreet by a Frank Kellett on January 24, 1886, are recorded in the Mohave County courthouse, Kingman, Arizona. Longstreet's worsening tax situation and the sale of his ranch to Wiser appear in the *Pioche Record*, August 6, 1887, September 22 and December 1, 1888. The ranching career of Wiser's daughter, Helen Stewart, who became the largest landowner in the area, is described in Carrie M. Townley, "Helen J. Stewart: First Lady of Las Vegas," parts 1 and 2, *Nevada Historical Society Quarterly* 16 and 17 (Winter 1973, Spring 1974): 215-44 and 2-32. For the candidates' letters, see Ed Pierson to Longstreet, October 18, 1888, James B. Wilson manuscript collection, Special Collections, University of Nevada, Las Vegas; and Maryellen V. Sadovich, "James Bernard Wilson—Forgotten Pioneer," *The West* 9 (October 1968): 65.

3

Sylvania

A lthough Lieutenant George Wheeler's topographic survey had passed through in 1871, the country into which Longstreet headed was still commonly known as the Unexplored Desert. The lines drawn on the maps showed that it was part of Nye County, Nevada, administratively linked to the dying mining camp of Belmont, where a few hangers-on still lived by the shriveled plums of political office that clung to a county seat. But Belmont lay far to the north, 140 miles and more away—long miles to a man on horseback—and its links with the "southern country," as this region was then called, were tenuous and occasional. Deputy Sheriff George Nicholl, setting forth on an exploratory foray into this domain in the spring of 1890, the year that traditionally marks the closing of the American frontier, rode past six new valleys, unnamed on any map he had seen. During his journey of the following year, Nicholl found only three white men living between 36.5 and 38 degrees latitude, an area comprising nearly 7,000 square miles.

One of these three was Jack Longstreet. He had recently taken up a small 160-acre homestead on the upper end of Oasis Valley, a narrow strip of brilliant green, about twelve miles long and half a mile wide, tightly cupped between low, rocky hills just north of present Beatty. The valley had been so named because it was an oasis in the literal sense of the

word, the first water in a hard forty-two-mile stretch for travelers coming in from Ash Meadows to the southeast.

Another early white settler in the valley at that time was
William Stockton, known as "the Old Man of the Desert."
The proximity of the Death Valley region made Stockton's
ranch a convenient encampment from which to pursue the
passion that had fired him for much of the past thirty years—
his quest for the legendary silver of the lost Gunsight ledge
and the elusive gold of the lost Breyfogle. These were obses-
sions of a kind that Longstreet wholeheartedly shared, and
long after Stockton had struck his pick into a ledge for the last
time, Longstreet would continue to ride out in search of the
lost Breyfogle.

In Oasis Valley Longstreet cut a little hay from the natural
meadowland and kept some horses and a few cattle. Unlike
the rich, level lands he had abandoned in the Moapa Valley,
the homestead probably could not have supported large operations. Even Deputy Nicholl, anxious though he was to ex-
tol the abundant resources and great virtues of the southern
country in hopes of encouraging settlement and railroad
building, was obliged to acknowledge that Oasis Valley contained little meadow and much rock.

Deputy Nicholl occupied himself by counting Longstreet's
twenty-eight stock cattle, eighteen horses, and one hog, and
evaluating his wagon at $25, also making mention of the
matter of $24.50 in taxes owed to the county. (Both Long-
street and Stockton had promptly appeared on the delinquent tax list.) Nonetheless, Nicholl received a warm welcome. The deputy sheriff reported that it would be hard to
find a "more friendly, sociable class of people" than the residents of the southern country. It was usually said of Longstreet that "everything he has belongs to a guest" and no one
ever dispensed warmer Southern hospitality. In those years,
however, his opportunities to welcome a traveler would have
been sparse indeed.

This Nevada Historical Society photo labeled "Longstreet Ranch, Amargosa Desert, 1907" may depict the Oasis Valley homestead

North of Oasis Valley lay the vast area designated Lava Fields on the maps, a region so desolate and godforsaken that even the Indians avoided it. In the language of the Nuwuvi, a desert such as this one was Yuwau-uk, "the hungry land," where even the ant will starve. Southward lay Death Valley, an eerily beautiful landscape of glittering white valleys, eroded golden mud hills, and dark, towering mountain heights. The Indians said it was made in the terrible cataclysm with which the gods punished the Paiute, Shoshone, and Mojave tribes for their incessant warfare. Molten lava poured upon the fleeing warriors, the earth quivered and cracked into chasms beneath their feet, a sea spilled through the mountains and dried into salt. The angry gods tossed the great mountain ranges—the Funerals, the Grapevines, and the Panamints—between their hands like soft clay, dropped rivers from the sky to harden them, then bent them and split them and set them on end. After taking all the rain away, they finally grew bored with destruction, but the desolate landscape remained as a punishment inflicted on man.

Many who take no stock in Indian legend had also found elements of punishment in Death Valley and its environs. Here the temperature has soared as high as 134 degrees in the summer. Swallows died in midflight and fell to earth. Sandstorms scoured the valley. Even after the wind died and a man could struggle to his feet once more, the blinding whiteness of the valleys and the heat haze could prevent him from seeing more than a hundred yards ahead. The madness that could overcome a traveler in the heat of the desert was said to begin with a roaring sound in his ears. His eyes would twitch, his pulse grow erratic, and commonly he succumbed to the hallucination that he was wading through deep water. Men sometimes died with canteens of water in their hands, in the belief that they were drowning. Even those who shunned all summer journeying did not fare well. Workers in the desert mines grew subject to fainting spells and turned quarrelsome and dangerous. Few lasted long in Death Valley and the southern country; those who did were a special breed of men.

They stayed on because they were the hardiest of the frontier survivors and they had no place else to run. From an early date the region had been a hideout for outlaws, rustlers, and bandits, including the stage robbers who fled from Pioche to the Panamints and discovered a rich silver mine. For years it was a local stage driver's custom to drop letters addressed to "John Doe" at Postoffice Spring near Ballarat and hang a rag on the creosote bush. When the coast was clear, nameless men hiding in the Panamints slipped out to claim their mail.

The venerable practice of raiding the peaceful, fertile valleys of California for horses continued to claim adherents among both Indians and newcomers. Some of the new residents of the southern country lived on small, shiftlessly run homesteads on the fringes of Death Valley like Longstreet's, and it is evident that they accounted for a disproportionate section of the Nye County delinquent tax list. Ralph J. ("Dad") Fairbanks, a subsequent neighbor of Longstreet's in Ash Meadows, told author Dane Coolidge that when he first settled on the fringes of Death Valley there were only five white men around, all "on the dodge for something" and most married to Indian women, although such unions were the object of public opprobrium and were forbidden by Nevada law. Out here beyond the edge of the civilized world, noted Coolidge, "there was absolutely no law of any kind." If some of these white fugitives from justice were killed by Indians from time to time, it was no matter of grave concern to Deputy Sheriff Nicholl in distant Belmont or to the scarcely less distant California law officers because "most of these men needed killing."

Longstreet was past fifty when he took up his Oasis Valley homestead. Ten years had passed since he came from the river in search of El Dorado, and none of them had been spent in so isolated a spot. Yet among these murderous desperadoes in a land so deadly that even old desert hands often perished on their journeyings, the aging frontiersman continued to survive, indeed to thrive like a thorned cactus perfectly adapted to its harsh environment. The Indians who accepted Longstreet as one of them, believed a man was identified by the land where his fathers lived since his race was created by the gods in the ancient days. Meeting another Indian, the Southern Paiute did not ask his name or the name of his tribe but rather "To what land do you belong? How are you land-named?" For Longstreet the answer was clear. He was land-named not by the steamy Louisiana bayous of his birth but by this savage desert country he had chosen for his own.

Around this time Longstreet was erratically pursuing another enterprise, in addition to keeping up the Oasis Valley homestead. In the mountains on the California-Nevada border northwest of Death Valley, the old mining camp of Sylvania, where lead and silver deposits had been discovered in 1873, was enjoying a minor revival. It was Longstreet's kind of camp—not a wealthy, civilized place like Virginia City, with opera houses, churches, fancy restaurants, gracious homes, and clubs where well-dressed men made rich by the Comstock gathered to discuss their financial speculations, but a small, rowdy camp, green with new hope, off on the edge of the known world, where a man with one ear slashed from his head could be accepted with no questions asked. Here Longstreet opened a tent saloon in which the overly rambunctious were restrained by the nudge of his gun.

Years later people still told of the night when a drunken cowboy strode in waving his six-gun. In no time a murderous brawl had blown up faster than a dust devil can twirl. Someone at the bar pulled his gun to shoot the newcomer, only to feel cold, steely pressure on his arm—Longstreet's gun barrel "making a point," in reporter Dave Toussaint's laconic phrase. When the cowboy tried to shake off the gun, Longstreet pulled the trigger and sent a warning bullet through the tent top. The sound of that shot is said to have had a wondrously calming effect upon the disputants. But how thoroughly perforated Longstreet's tent became in the course of keeping the peace in his saloon is not known.

In September 1890, he packed up his tent saloon and moved it from lower to upper Sylvania. Apparently the change was no improvement because Sylvania was inexorably sliding back into somnolence. Mining operations had already been sharply curtailed and soon would cease entirely, after exploration failed to uncover further ore deposits. Longstreet was not one to stay on watching the dust settle on the bar and listening to the wind whistle through the empty spaces. Knowing the smell of a ghost town in the making, he sold his portable saloon to Alexander Rampe, bundled his family into his wagon, and drove off toward Gold Mountain, where a new strike was rumored. The tent saloon at Sylvania was to be the last of the convivial enterprises that belonged to his middle years. Longstreet was turning now toward more solitary occupations, shunning even the raw young mining camps that used to pull him, and steadily withdrawing into ever more isolated country.

As usual, the current flowed the other way. Even old desert hands were fleeing the ranges of central and southern Nevada that winter. For some time, signs of increasing unrest among the Indians had alarmed the settlers of the region. Wovoka, the Paiute Ghost Dance messiah, living near the Walker River Reservation, had told the assembled tribesmen of his journeys to the land of the dead and had brought back messages from Numin'a, the Old Man who made the world. Wovoka taught them the sacred chants and the shuffling dance that they must perform with joined hands in concentric circles until they too fell to earth in trances like Wovoka's and walked with him in the land of the dead.

In 1888, after the sky had darkened with an eclipse, the Paiutes had seen Wovoka make the sun return. It was then that the Ghost Dance craze began to spread among the Indians of the West, many tribes sending ambassadors to hear the messiah's words and learn his teachings. Nevada's drought had ended, as Wovoka had promised, in a winter of massive snows. Rumors of more miracles passed from mouth to mouth. Wovoka had stood in fire without being burned; he had raised an old woman from the dead; his glance could melt boulders. Then had come his promise that in the spring of 1891 the grass would grow long and lush once more, the wild game would return to course the valleys, the old would become young, the dead warriors would live again, and Numin'a, the Old Man, would destroy the white man and restore the world to the Indian.

During the winter of 1890–1891 the messiah craze rose to fever pitch. Huge Ghost Dances were held, one near Independence, California, gathering at least 300 braves. The Nevada governor sent rifles and ammunition to Belmont;

men moved their families into the courthouse for safety and stood guard while the Indians danced in the Smoky Valley. On December 29 at Wounded Knee, Big Foot's band of Sioux was massacred in the Ghost Dance shirts they had believed would make them invulnerable to bullets, but this tragic news failed to dim the Nevada Indians' belief in the coming of the millennial spring.

The press reported the Indians "well armed and very saucy." Some spoke of the ranches, homes, and stores that would soon be theirs; others departed from their jobs without explanation. Prospectors who had walked unmolested and unafraid with their burros through the lonely reaches of the desert for years suddenly found it advisable to head into town for a while. They said the hills were alive with strange Indians and something was in the wind. Newly aware of their isolation and vulnerability in the heart of the Indian country, newspaper editors took to ruminating in print on how easily a town could be set to the torch on a windy night and its inhabitants "killed like rats in a hole." Military companies were formed in Hawthorne, Bodie, and the Mason Valley.

There was one man who did not ride into town for safety, having no cause to fear the Indians. He was, as one who knew him later said, "a master among them," and it was as a master that he led them in the one concrete gesture that this winter of fermenting expectations appears to have produced in the Great Basin. Longstreet was ultimately unable to turn his face away from the deepening discontent among the Indian miners whom he had come to know in the course of running his tent saloon.

At the Sylvania mine, Indian employees had long protested to no avail against Superintendent Robert Starett's refusal to pay them in cash or checks. They had instead been forced to accept blue scrip, which could be redeemed for cash only through the company's agents in San Francisco, obviously a near impossibility for an Indian miner, who was thus forced to trade with those merchants who would take the scrip and to accept any discount rate they cared to impose. For all practical purposes, the Indian miners had been paid with nothing more substantial than promises during the Sylvania Mining Company's last months of operation. It is not unlikely that Starett had employed Indians because white miners refused to work under these conditions. Longstreet had noted on his visits to Starett that the mine superintendent was well supplied with silver dollars. He apparently concluded that Starett's insistence upon paying the Indian miners in scrip was pure exploitation.

Matters moved toward a head soon after New Year's Day 1891, when Longstreet and a group of three Sioux runners and several Shoshone who had just participated in a grand Ghost Dance with the messiah at the Walker River Reservation arrived among the Indian laborers in the Palmetto-Sylvania region. The only other white man in the contingent was Ross Edwards, a Palmetto merchant married to an Indian woman and probably one of the Sylvania Mining Company's many creditors. By Sunday, January 4, according to a *San Francisco Examiner* account based on a letter from the superintendent of the Palmetto mine, a full-scale Ghost Dance was underway. Indians still on the job fled from work to join the large gathering on the crest of the White Mountains. There they joined hands with the rest and started circling rhythmically in the sacred dance, their chants occasionally punctuated by wild whooping.

When a heavy snowstorm blew in that night, the dancers on the peaks took shelter in the Palmetto mine. Apparently it was during this interlude of storm that Longstreet and Edwards turned the Indians toward the idea of forcing payment from the oppressive Starett. No doubt there were some who doubted that a group of almost unarmed Indians could force anybody to do anything, and some who denied the need of it, since the destruction of Superintendent Starett and all his kind and the restoration of the Indians' lost world was nearly at hand. Longstreet would have wasted no reliance on the promise of the millennial spring, well knowing that if the new hope that kindled his adopted people were to bring them anything more than an enlarged despair, they must act in the here and now. And in the end, they followed him. So it was that this one Ghost Dance ended not with the dancers falling to earth in hypnotic trances, not with memories of dreamlike journeys through the land of the dead, but with an outpouring of Indians led by Longstreet and Edwards.

The first stop was Home Rule Cabin, three miles away on the Tule Canyon trail. This was the abode of a tough Nova Scotian named Charles Murphy, who, as the press delicately phrased it, had been known to "persuade a stage to stop and surrender to an emergency," and his formidable old mother. About seventy-five Indians had been employed in Tule Canyon, some in Pigeon Springs on Murphy's *arrastras*, and Murphy had once paid a Shoshone laborer for a week's work with a stiff drink in lieu of the usual wage of a dollar a day. It had evidently been decided that the movement for fair pay should start with him, as he was judged capable of making recompense in liquor if not in cash.

They soon found that the stage robber was not to be easily parted from his dark bottles. On hearing a whoop from the crowd of Indians trampling the new-fallen snow outside his cabin, Murphy interrupted his Monday dinner of pork and beans, hid his bottle under the hearthstone, and fired his shotgun out the window. "Hand me the six-shooter," he told his old mother, and quickly sent six more shots toward the Indians outside. Several answering shots snapped back from the darkness, and Murphy reloaded in preparation for a rush on the cabin. But no rush occurred. Apparently the small grudge against him was judged not worth the bloodshed that would be the price of taking him, so the Ghost Dancers had moved on to their real quarry—Superintendent Starett.

As dawn cast a rosy tinge over the glittering new snow, they arrived at the Sylvania mine on a mountaintop just over the California border. Superintendent Starett, perhaps still asleep, was caught completely unawares when a small party led by Longstreet and Edwards stole into the cabin and abducted him. The crowd outside cut rods and beat Starett's naked flesh unmercifully until he agreed to make out checks to them for what the *Examiner* later termed "extravagant amounts." The interrupted Ghost Dance then resumed on the mountaintops, and liquor confiscated from the hapless Starett may have led some to deviate a bit from the usual prohibition against food or drink during the sacred ritual. Nonetheless, Longstreet and Edwards must have remained sober enough to see that Starett's checks were promptly cashed.

The next day Starett managed to pull his aching body onto a horse and start the long ride into town. In Independence he swore out warrants against Longstreet, Edwards, and several Indians. Meanwhile, Murphy organized a militia to resist further Indian trouble in the Sylvania area. The *Inyo Independent*, while acknowledging that Starett had sworn out a complaint against Edwards over a large check, denied that the superintendent had been molested by Indians. The *Examiner*'s version, however, was at least true to Longstreet's character. "The charge was highway robbery," the newspaper declared, "and the sheriff of Inyo County says the quest is useless, because Longstreet is a chronic case of refugee, and no Sheriff's posse has ever been able to corner him."

Possibly Longstreet found it wise to act on this strong hint from the sheriff and lie low until the storm blew over. News of his notorious doings disappeared from the press for a period of more than four years, perhaps for the good reason that he was entirely absent from the scene. It may have been during these years of silence, while he still had youth enough to range far, that Longstreet rode south toward the little town on the Mexican border and his next shooting. He tended to be vague about the date, only remarking in an offhanded way that it happened when "things were a bit quiet up here in Nevada."

Many years later he told *Tonopah Times-Bonanza* feature writer Eli Norton Richardson that there was just one man among those he had slain whose death might not have been entirely justified by the need to defend his own life. But that one was enough to leave him sleeping uneasy at night—even he, who some believed had no conscience at all and had long since grown inured to bloodshed and death. According to Richardson, he told the story in these words:

I killed them all in defense of my own life. There was one down in Arizona that has always bothered me—I have wondered if I did not make a mistake in bumping that fellow off. . . . I made a trip down to Arizona to take a look around. One day I rode into a small settlement not far from the Mexican border—I forget the name of the place—and, as was the custom in those days, I stopped in front of the first saloon I came to, threw the bridle over my cayuse's head and went in.

There were only two or three men in the place and as a sort of introduction I asked them to join me at the bar. One of them whipped out his gun. "All right," he said, "we'll drink with you but first you'll do a little dance for us." At that he took a couple of shots at the floor close to where I was standing—I suppose to make his demand more emphatic.

Well, I never was much of a dancer, so I took my poison and walked out. As I stopped to pick up the bridle and prepared to mount I turned around, and there stood the young fellow with his gun in his hand. I plugged him where he stood, right over the heart. Since then I have wondered if I was not a bit hasty. He was a young fellow and may just have been having some fun with me. I have never been able to decide whether the fellow was really in earnest or just joking.

I have always been bothered over that affair. Even yet that fellow comes to my bedside at night—often I can hear his voice plaintively asking, "Why did you kill me? I was just joking."

Notes

Deputy Nicholl's reports appear in the *Belmont Courier*, May 3 and 24, 1890, and June 13, 1891. Material on Death Valley and its environs has primarily been drawn from four sources: Dane Coolidge, *Death Valley Prospectors* (New York: Dutton, 1937), especially 45, 77–84, and 104–105; William A. Chalfant, *Death Valley: The Facts*, 3rd ed. (Palo Alto: Stanford University Press, 1930), especially 142–43; Bourke Lee, *Death Valley* (New York: Macmillan, 1930), especially Chapters 2 and 3; and John R. Spears, *Illustrated Sketches of Death Valley and Other Borax Deserts of the Pacific Coast* (Chicago and New York: Rand McNally, 1892). On Nevada's legal discrimination against Indians, see Hubert H. Bancroft, *History of Nevada 1540–1888* (San Francisco: The History Company, 1890), 160–62.

On Sylvania, see the *Inyo Register*, October 2, 9, and 30, 1890; the *Tonopah Times-Bonanza*, August 13, 1981; and Richard E. Lingenfelter, *Death Valley & the Amargosa: A Land of Illusion* (Berkeley and Los Angeles: University of California Press, 1986), 111, 339. Lingenfelter also traces the career of William Stockton on pp. 61–62, 69, 136, and 167. The Starett episode was reported in the *Inyo Independent*, January 16, 1891, and in the *San Francisco Examiner*, January 11, 1891. Mining operations in Tule Canyon are described in the *Chloride Belt*, December 17, 1890. Longstreet's Arizona reminiscence appears in the *Tonopah Times-Bonanza*, June 28, 1963.

4

Ash Meadows

Ash Meadows lies roughly forty-eight miles southeast of the Oasis Valley on the fringes of Death Valley, near the California state line. The Meadows' name derives from its velvet ash trees (now superseded by thickets of salt cedar), but the feature that chiefly distinguishes it from other mountain-ringed desert valleys in Nevada is the abundance of springs bubbling forth into blue-green pools teeming with tiny, silvery pupfish. No one knows the real extent of the maze of narrow connecting channels and large pools beneath the surface, and legends persist of bodies lost in one spring eventually surfacing in another.

East of the Meadows, beyond the mauve and cream-banded cones of the nearer mountains, tower the timbered, snow-capped heights of Charleston Peak. Due south, on the way to the Pahrump Valley, looms Shadow Mountain, strangely dark and mysterious in the midst of this bright landscape of mauve hills, dried golden saltgrass, aquamarine water, and white, mineral-encrusted earth. It is as though the mountain drew darkness like a magnet, gathering all the surrounding shadows onto itself. In the dust-colored desert at the base of the blue silhouette of the western mountains, the Amargosa River passes on its subterranean way to weave vaguely through the baking fastnesses of Death Valley and loses itself at last near Badwater in a pool with the steely gleam of a well-oiled gunbarrel.

Ash Meadows was the site of Longstreet's next appearance after the four year hiatus that followed the Ghost Dance lynching. The Oasis Valley place had been abandoned, and the spot he chose for his next ranch beside the spring that still bears his name was the scene of an early clash between Indians and whites. In 1849 emigrants seeking a shortcut across the desert to California had split off from a large wagon train traveling south to San Bernardino on the Old Spanish Trail. At Indian Springs, northwest of Las Vegas, one of these scattered parties not only raided the Southern Paiute fields of corn, pumpkins, and beans but also molested the Indian women. According to Ash Meadows Charlie, who still was war chief of the Ash Meadows Indians in Longstreet's day, the angry Indians attacked the emigrants as they camped at Longstreet Spring that night, shooting their oxen with arrows. This attack marked the beginning of the terrible sufferings the pioneers were to endure on their journey across Death Valley. News of their ordeal forestalled future attempts by emigrant parties to use this route and left Ash Meadows securely isolated in the desert.

One of the first ranchers to disturb its isolation was Charles King, a California gold rusher and a former guide with the 1871 Wheeler survey. In 1873 King ran a large herd of 1,300 cattle purchased in southern California in Ash Meadows and sold his beef at premium prices to miners at Ivanpah and the new rush just beginning in the Panamints west of Death Valley. But like most others, King was apparently unable to tolerate the southern country for more than a short spell. After only two years he sold out and moved on, leaving Ash Meadows to the murderous renegades who made it their own and to the Indians.

As King's short-lived enterprise had demonstrated, Ash Meadows, with its pulsing springs and level land, held much promise for a stock raiser whose tastes ran to isolation, but in the mountains to the southeast was something that may have attracted Longstreet rather more than the agricultural

Longstreet's stone cabin in Ash Meadows and Longstreet Spring in 1982. Timber for the long, thick ridgepole was probably hauled a considerable distance from the Spring Mountains. The mesquite thicket that formerly occupied the rise behind the cabin and the outbuildings have been bulldozed by subsequent owners (author's photos)

possibilities of the region. Here lay the Montgomery mining district, site of the Chispa mine and also of trouble and excitement of a kind that had been lacking on Longstreet's Oasis Valley ranch. For twenty years no one had been much inclined to believe that the western side of the Spring Mountains contained any gold worth fighting over. Prospectors had visited the area as early as 1869, but mining excitements had flared and died down in Palmetto, Lida, Gold Mountain, the Panamints, and other locales in the environs of Death Valley before the rush to Montgomery developed in early 1891.

The men who gave their name to the district and quickly emerged as its dominant figures were the Montgomery brothers, George and Earnest Alexander ("Bob" to his intimates). Because of their extensive mining activities in the Death Valley region during the years to come and Bob Montgomery's later eminence as the millionaire owner of the Montgomery Shoshone mine at Rhyolite, their backgrounds and even their appearances are better known than those of most desert wanderers. George was in his late thirties, dark-haired, blue-eyed, and a fine talker with an ability to convince others to invest in his mines—sometimes to their subsequent regret. Though Bob's wavy, slicked-down hair had turned prematurely gray, he was still only in his twenties. His picture shows a face with a long cleft chin, thick, twisted lips, and hard, unyielding eyes. Canadian born, two of seven brothers, George and Bob had abandoned their parents' Iowa farm in 1884 to seek their fortunes in the mining rush to Wood River, Idaho, with indifferent success. Fortune continued to elude George Montgomery on a prospecting trip with several companions for the lost Breyfogle in the Death Valley area during the winter of 1890–1891. Weary, discouraged, and on the verge of abandoning the quest, he had stopped to rest on his way back to camp when a nearby quartz ledge studded with gold nuggets like plums in a pudding happened to catch his eye. It suddenly appeared that George Montgomery's fortune was found after all.

George's initial elation at the discovery of the claim he named the Chispa (Spanish for "nugget") soon gave way to a prolonged search for capital to finance development of the mines. A visitor found "parties here are waiting and looking" but not as yet investing. The remoteness of the site posed enormous problems. All supplies had to be freighted in by wagon across the desert from Daggett on the Santa Fe Railroad 160 miles to the south, cramping construction and escalating prices. So few miners were available to work in such an isolated spot that it was necessary to pay them at the unusually high rate of $4 a day. A handful of enthusiasts declared themselves "sold on the country" and stayed on; most departed. Six months after the first rush, the camp boasted only men and not a single female resident. Pahrump rancher Harsha White, who visited Montgomery in September with a party including ladies, reported extensive preparations for a dance in celebration of this unique event: "All enjoyed themselves immensely until too tired to dance, too well served to eat and too sleepy to talk. All retired at a very late hour to rest for exercise the next day, which consisted of inspecting the mines."

Despite inspections such as these, all development at the mines spluttered to a halt in early 1892 amidst charges that George Montgomery's "extravagant management" was ruining his backers. A great deal of money had been squandered on an inefficient mill that recovered less than half the value in the Montgomery district's gold ores. Although the Chispa's gold veins were now generally dismissed as shallow and worthless, George headed for San Francisco in search of new backers to ruin. Soon the district was virtually abandoned. No mining was undertaken during most of the next two years, not even the minimal annual assessment work required by law to retain title to a mining claim.

One man not inclined to dismiss the Chispa's gold veins as shallow and worthless was Angus McArthur, previously foreman of the Garfield mines west of present Mina and more recently foreman of the Chispa. As McArthur gazed in the direction of the Chispa from the prosperous ranch he had purchased in the Pahrump Valley, a scheme was born that had nothing to do with the quality of the apricot crop, the size of figs, the progress of walnuts, the propagation of grapes, and other common preoccupations among the valley's horticulturists.

When McArthur learned that the Montgomerys had neglected the obligatory assessment work, he established his own claim upon the Chispa. The prize looked even richer when a new boom commenced in the Montgomery district in 1895. During the preceding winter, George Montgomery had finally found new backers. He sold the main interest in the district's two principal mines, the Chispa and the Johnnie, to the Sterling Mining Company, a Utah enterprise headed by Mormon leader Orson Smith. Another mill was brought in, and full-scale mining resumed in the district.

While the Chispa was now less vulnerable with a sizable force of miners on hand, McArthur went ahead with his plans all the same. Since the Montgomerys brushed aside his claim to the property, forceful action was needed. What McArthur had in mind involved the venerable principle that possession is nine-tenths of the law—his enemies called it "claim jumping"—and he knew exactly the men he needed to help him. At the tail end of an unusual summer, when eerily gorgeous sunsets blazed across the skies by night and the kind of heat that makes men mad as dogs suffused the desert by day, McArthur made his move.

In the ensuing events, which history remembers slightly askew as "the battle for the Johnnie," McArthur was said to have hired a private army of twenty-five men to win the mine. In fact, he appears to have hired but four. The first was Phil Foote, whom he offered a half interest. Foote, a former

gambler from Colorado, was recently embroiled with the law
for robbing a Salt Lake City gambling house and described
in the press as "nervy," perhaps in recognition of his success
in eluding arrest for a year before deciding to give himself up.
The others were Billy Moyer, George Morris, and an individ-
ual identified in the *Salt Lake City Tribune* as "Check Longstreet, a half breed." Yet the exaggerated press reports of a
private army had some basis in fact. As ominous rumors
about a "very serious state of affairs" began slowly trickling
back to Belmont, San Bernardino, and Salt Lake City, it
seemed that these particular four men could on occasion
fight like an army of twenty-five. Unfortunately for McArthur's future fortunes, the last phase of the battle at the
Chispa was not to be one of these occasions.

The first round went to McArthur's men, or the "professional fighters and desperate characters," as they were
termed in the press. At daybreak on August 28 they ousted
the Sterling guards and barricaded themselves at the Chispa.
Sterling's formal response was mild. President Smith declared that Sterling wanted the ownership issue adjudicated
and secured warrants from Belmont for the arrest of his op-
ponents. In fact, Sterling officials had no intention of waiting on the slow and uncertain processes of the law to win
back the Chispa, nor did the Montgomerys. George Montgomery was still part owner of the Johnnie in 1895, as well as its
superintendent, and a large unpaid debt he owed to McArthur
may have somehow figured in the dispute.

The Montgomerys swiftly assumed their posts as field
commanders of Sterling's forces in the district, dispatching
an agent to Los Angeles for two cases of rifles. A San Bernardino press account anticipated a long war of attrition for
control of the Chispa:

The men who are with MacArthur are a determined set,
and being led by a determined leader, a red-hot fight can be
looked for as soon as the Sterling Company's men return

with their rifles. The MacArthur contingent say they will
keep the mine and work it for all it is worth, while the Sterling men say they will have possession of it if it takes a
year's fighting to get it.

The country is said to be such that both sides can keep up
a long fight, with the chances of the outside parties being
able to succeed in starving the inside men out.

Possibly McArthur's men knew nothing about those cases
of rifles and were lulled into a false sense of security by the
expectation that the attempt to starve them into submission
would be a protracted one, while the wheels of the law ground
slowly away in distant Belmont. It was perhaps with some
such idea in mind that Longstreet had taken along his Indian wife to sweeten the dragging hours of confinement and
Foote had brought in a wagonload of supplies sufficient for a
long siege. At any rate, McArthur's force was caught completely by surprise only ten days after the seizure of Chispa
when a hired gunman, Peter Reed, and a crowd of miners led
by the Montgomerys attacked with rifles in the early morning. All were unarmed, with the probable exception of Longstreet. Foote crumpled with a bullet wound in his chest.

"Desperadoes Surprised—Volley is Poured into a Crowd—
Foote and Two Half-Breeds Fall—Posse of Twenty Deputy
Sheriffs on the Scene," read the hyperbolic headlines in the
Salt Lake City Tribune. Another version relates that Longstreet, realizing that the situation was hopeless and hoping
that Foote's life might be saved if the wound were treated,
hoisted his wife's white petticoat aloft over the Chispa as a
flag of surrender. Foote's wound nonetheless proved mortal.
Although doses of morphine eased his pain, he died that afternoon and received a fitting obituary from a Colorado
newsman: "He lived for the reputation of a dead game man
and he played the string out." Longstreet's own account of
the affair, when he arrived in Belmont under arrest on the
fourteenth of September, was typically laconic. He said that

Foote had been killed by "men from Montgomery" as he was starting to eat breakfast. Several shots had been fired, and no one else was hurt.

When the legal backwash of the Chispa affray at length rippled through the district court at Belmont, county officials had obviously decided that Sterling's cause was right and just and that McArthur's hired desperadoes ought to be punished. Determining the particular charges evidently posed a knotty problem because, now that Sterling had regained possession of the mine by force, company officials no longer found it desirable to raise the issue of McArthur's claim to ownership and he himself was not indicted. Nor was McArthur disposed to press his claim in court. Either he read the intended lesson in the battle at the Chispa and hastily backed off, or George Montgomery's debt to him was finally repaid.

The charge against Longstreet, Moyer, and Morris that Nye County District Attorney A. P. Johnson finally settled upon was "drawing and exhibiting a deadly weapon," a patently discriminatory pretext for legal action in an age when many men wore guns. Indeed officers could with equal justification have arrested Longstreet on any day of his adult life, because he was never seen on the range without his gun and is even said by some to have slept at night with a gun in each hand. No one was indicted for the killing of Phil Foote; law officers declared themselves unable to determine who had fired the fatal shot. Historian Richard Lingenfelter has pointed out, however, that the premier sharpshooter in the Montgomery force was Harry Ramsey, a Texan who had chiseled seven notches on his gun to commemorate the passing of the men who had killed his father and plundered his border saloon.

A poor and isolated region like Nye County in 1895 did not present a shining roster of legal lights from which McArthur could select a defense attorney for Longstreet, Moyer, and Morris. McArthur sent 150 miles away to Hawthorne for Patrick ("Patsy") Bowler, a former buckaroo who had taught himself law and served as district attorney of neighboring Esmeralda County. Bowler's bouts with the law in those days were intermittent, undertaken betwixt and between the pursuit of his mining enterprises. Before his death in 1916, he would gain a reputation for successfully defending more accused murderers than any other Nevada attorney of his day and would also blunder into certain disastrous legal fiascos. His defense of Longstreet, Moyer, and Morris was to be in the latter category, and it is clear that Longstreet formed a low opinion of his abilities.

On October 1 the three defendants were led from their jail cells in the rear of the neat, red brick Belmont courthouse to the courtroom in the front of the building. District Attorney Johnson set forth his case, aided by Peter Breen, an attorney of ultraconservative political views who would later become a district judge and had probably been hired by Sterling or the Montgomerys on this occasion to bolster Johnson's abilities. There was some cause to anticipate that Johnson might require bolstering. In the eyes of one of his successors in the Nye County district attorney's office, Johnson was an uncombed old muleskinner from Mosquito Creek with a stringy handlebar mustache, an unmistakable distaste for baths, and only a nodding acquaintance with the law.

Bowler, aided by a second attorney, W. N. Granger, had only to prove that drawing and exhibiting deadly weapons was a trumped-up charge under the circumstances, but the combination of the old muleskinner from Mosquito Creek and Breen proved too much for him. Before the sun slipped down over the rim of the Toquima Mountains, sloping skyward just behind the courthouse, the jury returned a verdict of guilty.

The punitive intent of the proceedings was crushingly affirmed by Judge J. A. Bell at the sentencing on the following day. Morris received a small fine of $25, commensurate with the crime. But Moyer and Longstreet were fined $450 and $300 respectively, plus all court costs. For misdemeanor charges, these were exorbitant sums, which neither man was able to pay. They languished in jail. Believing himself ill used and unwilling to tolerate it, Longstreet attempted to appeal, apparently without success. Toward the end of the month he was released, after posting an $800 bond, and rode south toward Silver Peak in the company of Morris, who had already been freed after serving out his sentence in lieu of paying his fine.

The affray at the Chispa had not yet run its full course, however. When the district court next convened in Belmont six months later, Longstreet was compelled to journey north from Ash Meadows to explain why his fine was still unpaid. He testified that he had given Bowler the money, but the attorney had neglected to turn it over to the court. Evidently Judge A. L. Fitzgerald believed him. Bowler was ordered to pay the fine within forty days or show cause. In fact, Bowler would not get around to paying the fine until April 1897, a year later. One day in the not too distant future Bowler and Longstreet would again encounter each other in the red brick Belmont courthouse, this time in the roles of prosecutor and prisoner accused of assault with intent to kill, but Longstreet would not again trust any cause of his to the legal ministrations of Patsy Bowler.

Years passed, memories turned wavery; in time the so-called "battle for the Johnnie" became part of the Longstreet legend, and the belief grew current that Longstreet had killed Phil Foote. People deduced this by the generally sound principle of logic that if someone were dead and Longstreet was present, he was the one responsible. All issues of claim jumping aside, Longstreet probably held himself responsible for a very different crime, possibly more heinous in the outlaw's code of ethics. The man whom everyone remembered as constantly on his guard, with gun at the ready, was unquestion-

ably guilty of insufficient wariness as he sat down to breakfast that September morning at the Chispa. He would not let
it happen again.

Nearly a month after Longstreet returned to his usual
haunts in Ash Meadows, the settlers scattered across Fish
Lake Valley and Tule Canyon south and west of the small
mining camp of Silver Peak were shocked by an unusually
brutal murder. The victim was a Yugoslav, locally called a
Slavonian in those days before the unification of Yugoslavia
as an independent nation in 1918. The killer was James
Boone, a forty-one-year-old West Virginian who kept a few
head of cattle and mined a little for the Yugoslavs on the side.
On the fatal evening, Boone had appeared in Bob Robinson's
Tule Canyon store and remarked that he expected trouble
with Antone Bacoch. When one of the customers asked him
why he was sharpening his knife on his boot, Boone replied,
"It's handy to have a sharp knife."

By the time Bacoch arrived at the store in his wagon, it was
nearly dark. Soon the two men were embroiled in a dispute
over an $11 debt. "I don't want any Slavonian son-of-a-bitch
to be my guardian," Boone told Bacoch, and Bacoch was not
slow to respond. He struck Boone with his fist and shoved
him through the door into Robinson's living quarters behind
the store. When Robinson worked up the courage to follow, he
saw the two men struggling on the bunk. Boone was plung-
ing his knife into Bacoch, while the Yugoslav's hand still
clutched his throat. Boone dropped the knife at Robinson's
urging, and Bacoch tumbled to the floor, expiring a few min-
utes later. His body was riddled with twenty-two stab
wounds.

No one made any move to impede the departure of the
blood-spattered fugitive as he saddled Robinson's horse and
rode away. He immediately headed for a cabin about a mile
away and sent a friend back to Robinson's store to collect $12
owed to him, which Robinson hastily paid. Taking this small

stake and $16 worth of gold dust, he galloped off into the November darkness.

Esmeralda County Sheriff William A. Ingalls, when apprised of this bloody killing, decided that he should remain in Hawthorne, where such urgent problems as liquor and opium sales to Indians demanded his immediate attention. Silver Peak Deputy Sam Wasson, more than eighty miles closer to the scene, took charge of the manhunt for Boone and called for the Indian trackers, a resource on which law officers often relied in especially difficult situations. On those rare occasions when the Indians failed to find their quarry, the press snidely derided them as "fakers." But let a particularly elusive prisoner escape from the state penitentiary, let a man lose himself in a desert blizzard beyond hope of rescue, then the Indian trackers were speedily summoned. In this instance, the trackers lost little time in picking up Boone's trail. Montezuma Dick, an Indian, later recalled the start of the manhunt in Tule Canyon: "After Antone die I try find Boone. Next morning I track him five miles. I track him until he change horses. I have rifle."

John Shakespeare, another Indian tracker, also gave his version: "Damn if I know when I last see Boone. Damn if I know how far I track him. He leave one horse, take nuthern. I got rifle. . . . Sam Wasson tell me bring Boone back."

As Shakespeare's words implied, Deputy Wasson had quickly abandoned the search for Boone. He disbanded his posse of Indians and settlers, explaining that the fugitive had headed into a region where pursuit was "almost impossible" because there were stretches forty to sixty miles long without feed or water. Otherwise, said Wasson, he would of course have followed Boone all the way to the Colorado. Many old desert hands would say that part about the long, dry stretches was an exaggeration, at least mostly, with just one or two exceptions, like the run from Oasis Valley to Ash Meadows. But it is entirely possible that Ingalls and Wasson felt less than enthusiastic about going forth in search of

Boone and perhaps actually finding him in some narrow defile out beyond the rim of nowhere, his clothes rusty with dried blood, sharpening his knife on his boot. They needed a man not likely to be fazed by danger, whether it came from the desert or a showdown with a killer who might fight like a mountain lion at bay. In short, it was time, and past time, to call for Jack Longstreet, and that is what they finally did.

No one appears to have questioned the propriety of sending a man with several notches on his gun, recently released on bail, on this mission as an agent of the law. To Longstreet's Indian companions, it probably seemed entirely appropriate, more so than many of the things they had watched the white men do. They knew that the hunter does well to poison his arrows with the blood of his quarry.

On the night of December 2, nearly two weeks after Boone took flight, letters from Longstreet arrived in Silver Peak by Indian courier. The following day Longstreet's message was relayed to Hawthorne and officials of the Carson and Colorado Railroad. The formal phraseology that appeared in the press was probably Wasson's rather than Longstreet's own: "Should he [Boone] reach the railroad, the fact that he is an old Southern Pacific engineer may help him to escape, but it is to be hoped that it will lead to his detection. . . . No more cruel deed was ever perpetrated in this country of outcasts . . . for Bacoch was unarmed and helpless at the time of the attack. I mention the fact of his being an old railroad engineer on the Southern Pacific, in hopes that those who are personally acquainted with him may help the officers of the law to apprehend him." Longstreet thought that Boone might still be hiding somewhere in the Amargosa Valley.

In fact, Boone was too canny to head for the railroad, and he had traveled fast. After the change of horses noted by the Indian trackers at the Ingalls mine, he had covered some ten miles to Oriental before noon of the day after the stabbing. The following day he was seen with blackened eyes, skinned hands, and bloody clothes at Amargosa, forty miles farther southeast. Apparently he did not pause again until he reached Stump Spring on the southwest edge of the Pahrump Valley forty-five miles below Longstreet's Ash Meadows cabin. There he somehow learned that Longstreet was on his trail. Exhausted though he undoubtedly felt after his desperate flight, he knew he could not linger. He "got a jack" and headed on south toward the Colorado. Either he succeeded in throwing Longstreet off his trail, as Longstreet's message to Silver Peak suggested, or the long lead he had already gained enabled him to make good his escape to Arizona, where he found work as a teamster. He now had a $950 reward on his head, $200 of it posted by John Chiatovitch, aged patriarch of the Yugoslavs in the Silver Peak region.

The denouement of the Boone affair came more swiftly than anyone anticipated. The following January, Yavapai County Sheriff George Ruffner used a cunning ruse to arrest him without a struggle as he drove his team down a desert road near Peach Springs. Had the news arrived a little sooner, the Yugoslavs would have turned out with greater zest to celebrate the traditional "big eat" on Christmas, the "big drink" on New Year's, and the round of festivities complete with fireworks, dancing, and dynamite explosions that began anew in January under the Greek Orthodox calendar.

Bacoch's nephew, leaving nothing to chance, hired two private attorneys from Carson City to assist the prosecution. Nonetheless, Boone's defense attorney, Patsy Bowler, arguing more effectively than he had done on Longstreet's behalf, convinced the jury in April 1896 that Boone had killed the unarmed Bacoch in self-defense. As he took his departure by a road that did not lead in the direction of the Yugoslav realm, Boone could count himself lucky, not only in his acquittal but also in the manner of his arrest. If he had to be found, better that Sheriff Ruffner should be the man to do it, rather than Longstreet, who was not past bringing in Boone the same way he brought in La Belle.

Longstreet returned to his white stone cabin beside the

spring in Ash Meadows. He appeared at Belmont only when the sheriff demanded his presence in court in connection with the protracted payment of his fine. What took place in Ash Meadows during the years from 1896 to 1899 is lost in the sun-drenched silence that enshrouded the remote southern country. Rumors of cattle rustling reached Belmont from time to time. A story is told in Ash Meadows of a protracted gunfight at Longstreet's cabin. His enemies failed to smoke him out because the water flowing from the spring inside his cabin where it backed against the hill enabled him to survive. But no one now remembers who these enemies were or why they waited outside the cabin through the days and nights to kill him.

When not engaged in fighting for his life, Longstreet is said to have primarily occupied himself with breeding horses, probably the fine thoroughbreds he consistently enjoyed. He would certainly have raced them from time to time, when a rancher in the Pahrump Valley, a miner at Montgomery, or an Indian thought he had a faster horse and wanted to prove it. If celebration seemed in order, it took the form of riotous drinking, of which a good deal went on in the Meadows. On these occasions, horses without racing qualities were often slaughtered and grilled over the Indian campfires.

There were two Indian camps nearby, one at the hill behind his cabin and the other farther northeast at Point of Rocks; both were linked to the Meadows by trails churned into deep dust by many comings and goings. We can be reasonably certain that Longstreet knew their inhabitants as well as he knew the white outlaws; so few people lived out there beyond the pale that it would have been impossible not to know them all, including the man he would one day have to kill and the last woman he would ever love.

Longstreet was undoubtedly acquainted with the Blacks, an Indian family in the Meadows. One of the Black women later married his good friend and drinking partner Albert Howell, a half-breed and an impecunious rancher. He surely knew the shadowy and dangerous Bob Black and once came near selling his ranch to the Indian. Bob's sister Fannie would also have been a familiar face to him. Whether Longstreet even then cast a warm eye on Fannie, with her high, jutting cheekbones, her full-lipped mouth, her long black hair, and her small, slender figure, is another mystery lost in the vast silences of the southern country.

Longstreet had other loyalties at that time. Cowboy Tex McCall used to tell about the day he rode up to the cabin at the spring. Longstreet greeted him and told him, "Get out and come on in. I want you to meet my new squaw." McCall was hospitably invited to "spend all night" if he wanted to. Longstreet may also have offered him a feast of some of Ash Meadows' more favored delicacies: bread made from mesquite beans ground upon a stone metate; a large, black chuckwalla lizard prodded out from his hole in the rocks by a sharp stick; or a mountain sheep hunted down at one of the waterholes in the western mountains and packed home to have the sinews pounded out of its flesh on a rock by Longstreet's new squaw, as the dogs whined at her heels for tidbits. A strong arm for pounding meat, shoeing a horse, or cranking a windlass was something that Longstreet prized in a woman a good deal more than simpering airs and prettifications. But, proud as he was of his latest bride in those years, the time would come when Longstreet would fight for Fannie Black.

Just then, though, he had another of his new beginnings in mind. In December 1899, he bought a new place, the Red Rock Ranch, though he still retained his Ash Meadows lands for several years. He was now sixty-one years old, still straight and strong, but the long blond hair that concealed his mutilated ear was turning gray. At an age when many men begin to think of resting for a while in the afternoon or moving south into the sun, he packed Susie, his Indian wife, into the wagon and headed north across the lava desert toward the Kawich Mountains.

Notes

On the history and ecology of Ash Meadows, see Coolidge, *Death Valley Prospectors*, 31–37; David L. Soltz and Robert J. Naiman, *The Natural History of Native Fishes in the Death Valley System* (Natural History Museum of Los Angeles County in Conjunction with the Death Valley Natural History Association, 1978), especially 3–5 and 34–39; Maryellen Sadovitch, *Your Guide to Southern Nevada* (Carson City: Nevada Historical Society Guide Book series, 1976), 24–25; and Lingenfelter, *Death Valley & the Amargosa*, 166–67.

Sources on the affray at the Chispa include the *Salt Lake City Tribune*, September 10, 1895; the *Walker Lake Bulletin*, September 18 and 25 and October 16, 1895; the *Belmont Courier*, September 14 and 21, October 5, 19, and 26, November 2 and 30, 1895, April 11, 1896, and April 17, 1897; "Annual Report of the Attorney General of the State of Nevada, 1895," in *Appendix to the Journals of the Senate and Assembly, 1897*, 34; and Lingenfelter, *Death Valley & the Amargosa*, 191–92. A largely inaccurate account also appears in Glasscock, *Gold in Them Hills*, 216–17. Bowler's most notable legal fiasco is recounted in Sally Zanjani and Guy Louis Rocha, *The Ignoble Conspiracy: Radicalism on Trial in Nevada* (Reno: University of Nevada Press, 1986). Additional background on the Montgomerys and the mining district that bore their name may also be found in Stanley W. Paher, *Nevada Ghost Towns and Mining Camps* (Berkeley: Howell-North Books, 1970), 324–26; Lingenfelter, *Death Valley & the Amargosa*, 189–202; and frequent issues of the *Belmont Courier*, especially the public letters from Henry Metz (dated April 22, 1891, in the May 9, 1891, issue), L. C. Morse (dated June 25, 1891, in the August 1, 1891, issue), and Harsha White (dated September 6, 1891, in the September 26, 1891, issue). On Bob Montgomery's background, see Bessie Beatty, *Who's Who in Nevada* (Los Angeles: Home Printing, 1907), 192–96.

The principal source on the manhunt for James Boone is the

Walker Lake Bulletin, November 27 and 30, December 4 and 11,
1895, and January 29, February 5, March 18, and April 29, 1896.
Additional background on the Yugoslavs appears in the January
15, 1896, issue; in Hugh A. Shamberger, *Silver Peak* (Carson City:
Nevada Historical Press, 1976); and in Leonore M. Kosso, "Yugoslavs in Nevada, Part I," *Nevada Historical Society Quarterly* 28
(Summer 1985): 69-73. Material on Longstreet in Ash Meadows
1896-1899 was drawn from oral interviews with George Ishmael
(November 2, 1982, March 1, 1983), Noreen Rooker (February 20,
1982), and Pete Petersen (February 20, 1982), and from the *Belmont
Courier*, October 10, 1896, and December 9, 1899.

5

Red Rock Ranch

Red Rock Ranch lay deep in a curling canyon in the Kawich Mountains about forty miles southeast from present Tonopah. Hemmed in on three sides by the pinon and juniper-studded mountain heights, invisible from the valley beyond, it had the qualities of a hidden fortress. Long rock walls ascended the canyon slopes, and the southern front of the sod-roofed stone dugout was constructed four feet thick. The canyon was less practical for raising stock than Ash Meadows, with its well-watered meadows and its level cropland, and far less desirable than the prime ranch abandoned a decade earlier in the Moapa Valley. But it was also less exposed, the kind of place that could serve a purpose more important to Longstreet than ranching. A sense of drawing in, crouching down, and taking cover clung to Red Rock Ranch.

Beyond the flaming cliff that gave the ranch its name, the broad, treeless waste of Cactus Flat merged into the Stone Cabin Valley to the north. From the pale green expanse of rabbitbrush, shadscale, and sage that covered the valley like a smooth, unbroken mantle, submerged hills struggled to rise at the rim of the Kawich, their rose-colored tips bursting through the surface, then cresting even higher into the slate blue heights of the range.

More than eighty miles to the northwest lay Belmont, blowing down and crumbling away beneath the great bowed arch of the mountain, as it had done for more than a decade.

The Kawich Mountains near Red Rock Ranch (author's photo)

The dismemberment of depopulated Nye County among the neighboring counties had been seriously discussed at the last session of the Nevada legislature. And for good reason. Nye County seemed bereft of any just claim to continued existence. Its ranges were stripped by overgrazing of the once-lush Indian rice grass and white sage, its mines played out, its population fled, save for the last few hangers-on, most of them sporadically prospecting on the side, whatever their nominal occupations, in the same desultory and supplemental way that their wives kept little vegetable gardens and a few hogs. No one in this forgotten frontier backwater could indulge in the luxury of an illness or a hasty marriage, for the town boasted neither a doctor nor a preacher. Such matters had to await the annual visit of the Chinese doctor of herbal medicine from Carson City or the occasional evangelist. The *Belmont Courier* was so starved for news that the editor was reduced to reporting such events as the diminishing size of winter woodpiles and the appearance of a wounded bird like a giant owl with a cat's head, which hunters called a "musk-cat." The creature had materialized in someone's corral like a mysterious portent.

None could then know, as Longstreet's team creaked slowly across the empty miles of Cactus Flat, that within the year Jim Butler's discovery of silver at Tonopah would ignite a boom that was to transform the central Nevada landscape, spawning a host of new mining camps throughout the region. Inside seven years, Rabbit Springs, where Longstreet may well have paused to water his team and seen no other sign of life than the spurting dash of a rabbit between the Joshua palms, was to be a city of some 20,000: Goldfield, the site for a few glorious years of some of the richest gold mines in America.

But the raging December wind that howled across Cactus Flat, sending the cattle huddling into the draws for shelter and frosting the fawn-colored backs of the antelope with snow, brought no hint of the changes so soon to come. In December 1899, the population of the region south of Belmont on the fringe of the Unexplored Desert was still counted not in the thousands but on the fingers.

Longstreet had no near neighbors in the Kawich. Even his distant neighbors were few and far between. Westward more than fifteen miles across the celadon emptiness of Cactus Flat was the ranch where a tall, laconic cowboy, Orville K. Reed, always known as O. K., lived with his brother. Reed was to remain Longstreet's friend for nearly thirty years. About six miles south of Red Rock Ranch stood the sod-roofed stone and adobe buildings of the cattle ranch belonging to Richard Breen, a bachelor Irishman of about fifty years who had lived long in the Kawich. How well Longstreet knew him is hard to say, but it seems to have been well enough for Longstreet to be angered by the terrible way he died.

Some twenty miles northward was the Clifford place at

Stone Cabin. The patriarch, Irish-born Edward Clifford, was then forty-eight years old, short and stocky, with the brawny build of a former coal miner. He had worked in the mines in Maryland, Wyoming, and Colorado, before heading farther west in a wagon train with his wife, Esther, and their two little sons. After trying his luck in Austin and Tybo, he became the foreman at the Spanish Belt mines but soon abandoned the job to homestead in the Stone Cabin Valley. There he gathered around him something that the lonely, childless Jack Longstreet would never have, for all his fondness for children and his fathering of the desert waifs cast on his doorstep by chance or tragedy—a large and affectionate family. In 1899, nine of the eleven children Esther Clifford had borne to Ed were still living, and two of them, Edward Jr. and the big, ruddy, freckle-faced James, were already full-grown men of twenty-six and twenty-four who rode the range with their father. And fought beside him too, when the time came.

Together these Cliffords were a powerful and respected force in the community where they had pioneered for nearly twenty years before the blond, long-haired stranger rode in from the southern country. Never a wedding, never a dance in Belmont's old Cosmopolitan Saloon, never an annual Fourth of July picnic in Pablo Canyon took place without them. Scarcely an issue of the *Belmont Courier* went to press without relating their sociable comings and goings. They had earned their place, and if they had come to see the land east of the Monitor range and west of the Kawich as their own preserve, they had good reasons for doing so.

No one is entirely sure why matters between Longstreet and the Cliffords had arrived at a shooting stage a little more than two years later. Ed Clifford was, as the *Tonopah Bonanza* gently phrased it, "wary of making new friendships or taking strangers into his counsels," yet there must have been a good deal more to it than that. Longstreet had his own story, and it was an ugly one. Some believe the quarrel started in a "horse deal," for Longstreet had brought his passion for breeding and racing fine horses with him to the Kawich. The Cliffords' descendants think the rift had to do with disputes over mining claims, which would certainly have been considered worth fighting over in the Longstreet lexicon, or with Longstreet's theft of a Clifford beef to improve his table. And that, too, is not entirely implausible, as the sage hens were sometimes scarce and the deer and antelope fleet. Longstreet, now far removed from those tasty feasts of chuckwalla lizards and mountain sheep that had assuaged the hunger of the Indians and the settlers in Ash Meadows, might not have been past finding a more piquant flavor in the beefs of an enemy than he did in his own.

Whatever the cause, the rift widened. Longstreet stayed well within his mountain fastnesses, avoiding the neighborly scrutiny of the *Belmont Courier* and brewing his quarrels in secret. In July 1901, *Courier* readers were assured: "The reported death of Jack Longstreet is false in every particular. Jack is still in the land of the living and in good health." Whether Longstreet had merely been ill or had come close to departing the land of the living in a gunfight was not explained. Apart from this cloudy report, the *Courier*'s news centered upon such momentous events as an attack of rheumatism and a finished haystack. No further public hints of the murderous feud germinating in the Kawich rippled the somnolent surface of life in these last days of Belmont, a town so drained of juice that whole sessions of the district court sometimes passed without a single crime to consider and the sheriff felt free to depart for a two-month vacation in southern California. All this would abruptly change on the February day in 1902 when Longstreet went rampaging through Tonopah after the Cliffords.

He caught up with Ed Clifford, Jr., in the Tonopah Mining Company office. Harsh words were exchanged, and Longstreet drew his pistol. In the ensuing scuffle, manager Tasker L. Oddie (the future Nevada governor and U.S. Senator) and superintendent Fred Siebert succeeded in disrupting his aim so that the shot intended for Clifford rocketed wildly through a board partition into the floor. It must have given the Cliffords considerable pleasure to have Longstreet arrested for intent to kill and placed under a heavy $2,000 bond. The time was past, however, when fines or bonds could be used to deny Longstreet his freedom. His financial affairs had apparently undergone considerable improvement during the seven years since he had languished in the Belmont jail unable to pay his fine. He posted the bond in short order. Soon he was back in the Kawich, angrier than ever. As one long-time resident of Tonopah has remarked, "Sometimes people tried to walk over Longstreet, but he never allowed it." Just then, the Cliffords were walking a little too close.

The next encounter between Longstreet and the Cliffords came three weeks later on March 11, an unseasonably cold, raw day. Enough snow had fallen to whiten the far peaks so that they billowed over the horizon with the unearthly purity of spirit mountains belonging to a different realm than the ash-gray plains beneath. Joe Nay, husband to Ed Clifford's daughter Ellen, had neglected to bring warm clothes along for their visit to his wife's parents at Stone Cabin. Before riding out with Ed and James that day, he borrowed a hat, coat, and chaps from his father-in-law. It appears that, on Ed's urging, he may also have borrowed his father-in-law's usual saddle horse. The Clifford party rode very far that day, perhaps a good deal farther than Ed's ranch work demanded. Five o'clock found them still more than twenty miles from Stone Cabin, at the point behind the dome-shaped hill like the crown of a ten-gallon hat where the trail turned back toward the ruddy cliffs of Longstreet's mountain fortress.

The Cliffords claimed that they unexpectedly came upon Longstreet, dismounted and carrying a gun, accompanied by Jim Smith. They immediately leapt from their horses. Longstreet fired two shots at them, one raising a blood blister under James's nose and the other striking Joe Nay's left knee as he hurriedly slid from his horse. James fired two shots in return, one of which wounded Smith's horse in the shoulder. No further shots were fired. Longstreet and Smith had quickly taken cover in a small ditch; Ed and James Clifford hid behind the rimrock, dragging the wounded and helpless Nay in beside them. There they waited, eyes straining in the last light of the dying day, for a telltale sign of movement. After dark Longstreet and Smith crept silently along the ditch and over a hill. Amidst the pinon and juniper trees, they found their horses waiting patiently in the darkness. Then they rode hard for the canyon road and home. Meanwhile, one of the Cliffords rode to Stone Cabin for a buggy in which to bring home the wounded Nay. When they finally carried her husband into the house many hours later, Ellen found his boot filled with frozen blood.

Jim Smith subsequently told the *Tonopah Bonanza* a considerably different story about who had fired first. Smith said that he had lost a glove while looking for stock with Longstreet. They were riding along a wash hunting the lost glove when Longstreet spotted it, rode ahead, and dismounted to pick it up. Just then the Clifford party came suddenly galloping over the rise, leapt from their horses, and fired at Longstreet, the second shot passing over his head as he sprang into the gully. After Longstreet sent two answering bullets in their direction, the Cliffords aimed a shot at Smith, who was at least forty feet from the line of fire and had taken no part in the affray. It struck his horse in the shoulder, causing it to stumble and throw Smith. He had then followed the little gully to the spot where Longstreet crouched, his gun at the ready, and lain down beside him.

If Smith spoke the truth, it was clear that Longstreet's rumored prowess with his gun was no exaggeration. He had dodged the Clifford bullets with an agility that few men of sixty-four years could match. Though taken by surprise and compelled to fire quickly over a considerable distance, he had struck one target and grazed the other with the only two shots he had fired. Some people believe that if Longstreet had been shooting to kill, Nay would have been a dead man, a view that some of the Cliffords themselves might not have disputed. Tom, one of the younger Clifford brothers, later acknowledged, "Longstreet was the best shot with a pistol you ever saw."

The following morning Deputy Sheriff Pat O'Brien, Justice of the Peace Clay Peters, and Mike Sheridan, superintendent of the Tonopah Company mines, examined Smith's wounded horse, an important piece of evidence in the trial to come. They also walked over the rimrock, the sandy gully, and the buff-colored hill, shading to rocks of cream and rouge at the crenellated crest. The footprints, the turned stones, and the disturbed earth bore witness that indeed men had fought here not many hours ago. But there was nothing in the blue stillness, fragrant with sage and pinon, to tell who it was that had ridden out looking for a man he meant to kill.

In a private letter to his mother, Nye County District Attorney Tasker Oddie grimly observed that Longstreet and the Cliffords "make things interesting for each other & some of them will be killed soon." Longstreet was once more arrested. It may have been then that he learned for the first time that the man wearing Ed Clifford's clothes whom he had shot was not Ed Clifford but young Joe Nay, to whom he had wished no harm. At best Nay would be crippled for life, and at worst he would lose his leg. It was a sobering realization, perhaps no less for the Cliffords than for Longstreet. Despite the district attorney's forebodings, no further shooting occurred between them after Longstreet was released on a $3,000 bond following his preliminary examination.

It may well be that the Cliffords counted on the law to punish Longstreet so severely that, when he finally got out of jail some years hence, he would pack his squaw into his rig and head back into the Unexplored Desert, to wherever it was he had come from. After all, this was old Ed Clifford's place. The men from whom the jury would be chosen were his neighbors of twenty years, not a few of them related to him by the marriages of his sons and daughters. Although they had their share of fights and feuds, the Cliffords were woven into Belmont as tightly as a willow whip in a Shoshone water basket. And what was Longstreet? Many might share the critical assessment that pioneer editor Carl B. Glasscock was later to deliver: "Violent, morose and vindictive, he [Longstreet] was feared and hated by all the widely scattered ranchers on the desert. He was generally looked upon as a cattle and horse thief, but with a reputation for such efficient gun-play that few dared make trouble for him." Moreover, he was a stranger with a shadowy past who kept to himself, known to Belmont only as the claim jumper they had jailed after the gun battle at the Chispa. How could an outsider of such repute match a Clifford's claim to the loyalty of the community?

Longstreet may have harbored a similar assessment of his situation as he set about engaging not one but three attorneys with considerably more care than he had shown following the Chispa affray. One was his former defense attorney, W. N. Granger, of whom the district attorney had privately observed, "he is an old scamp and is always drunk." But his additional selections of a future Congressman and a future U.S. Senator suggest that he was developing nearly as discriminating an eye for lawyers as for fine horseflesh. The future congressman was George A. Bartlett, a thirty-two-year-old Eureka attorney who was contemplating seeking his fortune in Tonopah. After a preliminary foray with a friend, Bartlett wrote to his father in May, "I am becoming strong in the faith that my only salvation also lies in Tonopah." Bartlett's salvation commenced with the representation of the long-haired frontiersman. One day, in his own way, Longstreet would return the favor.

Longstreet's third attorney was Key Pittman, who a decade later would assume the Senatorial seat that he was to retain for more than a quarter of a century. In the spring of

1902, he was a twenty-nine-year-old Southern-born adventurer, just down from the Yukon. While awaiting employment in lucrative mining litigation, Pittman found it difficult to raise the $200 necessary to build a cabin in Tonopah. He was worried that, as he expressed it in a letter to his wife, Mimosa, "I don't believe the people here know I am a lawyer." As a result, he was happy to assist in Longstreet's defense, even though he apparently regarded it as a hopeless cause. Longstreet, for his part, may have ascertained that Pittman was a brilliant attorney when sober.

Longstreet was presently indicted by the grand jury for assault with intent to kill Nay, but no true bill was returned for his attack upon Ed, Jr., in Tonopah.

The trial opened in Belmont on June 19 and was afterward remembered as the last great trial ever held in the old red-brick courthouse before the county seat shifted to booming Tonopah. Wild roses were blooming and doves were fluttering in the mountain canyons under a blazing sun as attorneys, witnesses, and interested spectators rode north through the broad Monitor Valley toward the spot where the brushy green heights of the Toquima Mountains on the western rim dissolved into a series of rocky, conical hills at the valley floor. Pittman, in a topless buggy, took a keen, if slightly reckless, pleasure in pulling ahead of the prosecutors' crack team and deluging the party with a cloud of dust.

On the edge of Belmont the tall, coral-brick chimney of the old Monitor-Belmont mill kept watch like a grave market over the dying town. The way led on, past the sagging board porch of the Cosmopolitan Saloon, where opera singers had appeared in better, flusher times and where the whole town, and most of the county, had turned out less than three years ago for the dance that followed the wedding of Ellen Clifford and Joe Nay. The courthouse, with its high arched windows and its white cupola, its old brick ruddy against the gray sagebrush, stood on a rise west of the Cosmopolitan at the base of the mountains. It was rumored that one of Long-

Future U.S. senator Key Pittman in the early days when his brilliant defense of Longstreet helped to establish his legal credentials in Nevada (Nevada Historical Society)

street's friends waited nearby with a string of swift horses, bridled and ready, just in case the trial went badly. Pittman also sensed a disaster in the making. "Don't think worse case will be tried this term," he wrote hurriedly to his wife.

Matters commenced promisingly for Longstreet, nonetheless. He would have noted with satisfaction that the prosecution was not being conducted by District Attorney Oddie, as had originally been planned, but by R. L. Johns, the deputy district attorney, and by Special Counsel Patsy Bowler, his former defense attorney under whose auspices he had been convicted for the only time in the last twenty years. The ethics of Bowler's presence as a special prosecutor against his former client were decidedly questionable, and the rift between the two of them that had accompanied Bowler's prolonged procrastination in turning Longstreet's fine over to the court may well have lent an extra edge of animosity to the proceedings. Added to this was the budding rivalry between Pittman and Johns. After besting the deputy district attorney in his first Nevada trial two months earlier, Pittman had noted that Johns was "quite sore and seems to take it personally."

As the prosecutors questioned the prospective jurors, it became clear that they faced a more formidable assignment than anyone had probably anticipated. Jury selection dragged on through the entire day because one venireman after another had to be excused when he declared himself convinced of Longstreet's innocence. Despite these hopeful signs, Pittman remained pessimistic. He wrote his wife that the jurors would be bad for Longstreet and the best outcome he could envisage was a hung jury.

When the time finally arrived for the prosecution to commence its presentation, Pittman's pessimism appeared justified. The jurors could not help reacting sympathetically when Joe Nay was carried into the courtroom, the odors from his wounded knee wafting to every nose with the suggestion of a life tragically ruined at the age of thirty. Twelve witnesses for the prosecution took the stand, six of them members of the Clifford family. They claimed that Longstreet had killed a steer belonging to them in February and carried away a hindquarter. Fearing prosecution as a cattle thief, he had "premeditatedly" waylaid the Clifford party and shot to kill.

Their story was swiftly dismantled by Key Pittman in a series of brilliant cross examinations, which undoubtedly did a good deal to establish him as a lawyer in the public eye. The handsome, clean-shaven young attorney, his dark hair combed smoothly back from a widow's peak, rose to his feet, providentially sober, fixed his large, slightly wild brown eyes on the Cliffords, and proceeded to demolish their stories. He may have wondered why they happened to be twenty miles from Stone Cabin near Red Rock Ranch at five o'clock on a bitterly cold winter afternoon if they were not hunting Longstreet. He may have questioned why Longstreet would have chosen a small gully where the Clifford gunfire could easily pin him down as the site for the alleged ambush. He might have noticed a certain discrepancy in Longstreet's alleged desire to risk prosecution on a murder charge in order to avoid prosecution as a cattle thief. Soon the prosecution witnesses were stumbling into what the press termed "frequent contradictions" that tended to "destroy faith in the truth" of the Clifford position.

When the defense attorneys commenced their presentation the following week, the momentum grew even stronger. Jim Smith's wounded horse was introduced into evidence, and four defense witnesses appeared, apparently including Sheriff Thomas Logan. A former resident of the Moapa Valley, Logan must have known Longstreet since the 1880s. The Cliffords considered that the sheriff's favorable testimony lent him little credit. As Nay's daughter Leafy later said, "Even the officers were scared of Longstreet. He had them all buffaloed. They knew they'd be the next notch on his gun."

Longstreet himself took the stand, his long, graying blond hair concealing the mutilated ear, his manner still showing traces of Southern courtliness, and told his story in a soft drawl. Smith and he had been looking for stock near Red Rock Ranch when the Clifford party suddenly appeared over a little rise about 300 yards away, galloping rapidly toward him. At a distance of about 150 yards, they dismounted and shot twice at him, one bullet tearing up the dirt at his feet. He had fired back at the only man of the Clifford party who had not taken cover. The defense attorney then inquired about the reason for the Cliffords' attack.

Longstreet's answer led back to the days when he had first moved into the Kawich, and brought to the surface the ugly story that had coiled beneath the feud like a rattlesnake under a stone. It had started around three o'clock on the morning of January 13, 1900. Longstreet had been roused by an Indian boy sent by Ed Clifford, Jr., and his brother James to summon him to the Breen ranch. On his arrival, the Cliffords related that they had grown concerned when they stopped by the ranch and found their old friend's door unlocked and his house empty. They had searched for hours in the dark until they found Breen's bruised and mangled body lying in the meadow. They had then sent for Longstreet, Breen's nearest neighbor. While Longstreet and Ed, Jr. remained with the body, James rode to inform Sheriff Logan in Belmont.

After examining the tableau at the ranch, Sheriff Logan was not convinced that Breen's death had been a terrible accident, and the ensuing coroner's inquest recommended a grand jury investigation. Probate of the will, in which Breen had left his ranch and stock to Ed, Jr., was presently challenged by Nye County Public Administrator Charles W. Anderson on the ground that the will was a "forged and fraudulent instrument." Anderson had accompanied Sheriff Logan, James Clifford, and Joseph McCann on their journey from Belmont to the Breen ranch with the coffin. It is impossible to avoid the observation that of the four men outside the Clifford family who viewed the scene of the tragedy, at least three—Longstreet, Logan, and Anderson—believed there was something very suspicious about Breen's will, or his death, or both.

In time, the courts decided otherwise. The grand jury that convened in April 1900 heard witnesses describe the circumstances at the Breen ranch. Several horses and a mule with a long rope tied around its neck had been seen feeding in the meadow where Breen's body was found. Two coyotes, a horse, and a dog, all dead, also lay in the meadow. Footprints suggested that Breen had walked about wearing only one boot, then gone barefooted. The grand jury concluded that the solitary Irish rancher was "of unsound mind, and came to his death through wandering around, and from exposure."

More than two years were to pass before the Breen will controversy was eventually settled in the Cliffords' favor. Anderson's objections were voided in 1901 because they had been filed five days too late, and he eventually agreed to withdraw them. However, at the time of Longstreet's confrontations with the Cliffords in February and March 1902, the legal judgment on the Breen will was still hanging fire. Not until the day that Longstreet's own trial commenced did District Judge Benjamin Curler finally render his decision that the Breen will was genuine. On this and other occasions, both in and out of court, the Cliffords' long friendship with Breen undoubtedly spoke in their favor. Yet, despite all legal vindications, the rumors persisted, because the grand jury's verdict of death from madness and exposure had failed to satisfactorily explain the condition of Richard Breen's body. He was terribly bruised, his elbow was lacerated, the flesh was worn off one toe to the bone, and his neck was broken.

Now, under his attorney's questioning, Longstreet again told the story he had refused to swallow in silence, whatever the courts decided. His belief, corroborated in court by Sheriff Logan's testimony, was that someone had murdered Richard Breen by dragging him to death behind a horse, and the guilt pointed strongly to Ed and James Clifford. Breen's will leaving his ranch to the Cliffords was a forgery written out by the Cliffords themselves. All this he knew, said Longstreet, his eyes flashing ice blue at the Cliffords, and he had not been afraid to say it. Prior to the gunfight in the Kawich, the Cliffords had threatened to kill him unless he ceased talking

about Breen's mysterious death and the forged will. In closing arguments, the defense attorneys boldly offered to prove
the Breen will a forgery.* It was beginning to seem that the
Cliffords were on trial rather than Jack Longstreet.

The jurors retired. At eleven o'clock they asked to have
Longstreet's testimony read to them. Two hours later they
had reached a verdict: not guilty. Subsequent inquiries about
their decision by the *Tonopah Bonanza* revealed that the
contradictions brought out during cross examination had
destroyed the credibility of the Cliffords' story, "as did also
the improbability of the killing of the steer imputed to Longstreet." Alice Lorigan, who knew him for years, later summed
up the opinion that the jurors and many others had apparently formed of Longstreet: he could kill a man, but "He
didn't do the starting."

Longstreet must have visibly relaxed. There would be no
need for the hand-picked relay of his swiftest horses. Instead
of making a dash at gunpoint and fleeing into the world
beyond the pale where he had learned so well to hide, there
would be time to stroll across the road and lift a glass or two,
to receive the congratulations of friends and savor for an afternoon the knowledge that, in spite of his lonely ways, his
shadowed past, and his branded flesh, he had won a kind of
acceptance in this place. His word was good. Perhaps here,
on the fringes of the last great boom of the dying frontier,
where the air reverberated once again with the old excitement that had quickened his blood for years, his restless
wanderings had finally reached an end.

Notes

Red Rock Ranch was also sometimes called Hawes Canyon
Ranch. The site now appears on Bureau of Land Management maps

---

*No evidence has been uncovered substantiating the Anderson-
Longstreet allegations concerning the Breen will.

as Longstreet Canyon and Longstreet Ranch. Details on life in the area were drawn from the *Belmont Courier.*

Longstreet's affrays with the Cliffords appear in the *Tonopah Bonanza*, February 22, March 15, March 22, June 21, and June 28, 1902, and the records of his trial at the Nye County courthouse, Tonopah, Nevada. Some interesting details are also noted by Thomas W. Miller in "Memoirs of Thomas Woodnut Miller, a Public Spirited Citizen of Delaware and Nevada," (Reno: University of Nevada Oral History Project, 1965), 57. Additional information on the Cliffords is found in the U.S. censuses of 1900 and 1910, and the *Tonopah Daily Bonanza*, April 14, 18, and 19, 1916.

On Richard Breen's death, see the *Belmont Courier*, January 20, April 14 and 21, 1900, and the records in the Breen probate file at the Nye County courthouse. Material on Longstreet's attorneys has been drawn from Fred L. Israel, *Nevada's Key Pittman* (Lincoln: University of Nebraska Press, 1963), especially 7-18; the *Reno Gazette-Journal*, September 9, 1979, 2A; the George A. Bartlett Papers, Special Collections, University Library, University of Nevada, Reno, especially Bartlett's letter to his father dated May, 1902; the Key Pittman Papers, Library of Congress, Washington, D.C., especially Key Pittman to Mimosa Pittman, April 9 and 12, June 19 and 22, 1902, Box 53; and Evelyne Wash-Pickett, "Tasker Oddie in Belmont," *Nevada Historical Society Quarterly* 29 (Summer 1986):93. Tasker L. Oddie's activities in this period are briefly touched upon in Loren B. Chan, *Sagebrush Statesman: Tasker L. Oddie of Nevada* (Reno: University of Nevada Press, 1973), 25-28. Also see Tasker Oddie to Ellen Oddie, February 24 and March 20, 1902, Tasker L. Oddie Papers, Nevada Historical Society, Reno. Further material on Thomas Logan appears in Phillip I. Earl, "Murder Helped to Boost Fortunes," *Apple Tree* (February 1, 1981), 2, and Dorothy Mason and Allen Metscher, "The Killing of Sheriff Logan," *Central Nevada's Glorious Past*, 3 (November 1980).

Oral sources for this chapter included Joseph Clifford (August 1980, August 1981) and Olephia ("Leafy") Nay King (August 20, 1982), both grandchildren of Edward Clifford; Buster Fillipinni (March 31, 1983), a great-grandson; Alice Lorigan (March 31, 1983); and Austin Wardle (March 30, 1983). King has also described these events in "Dust and Desire, Laughter and Tears: Recollections of a Nevada Pioneer Cowgirl and Poet" (Reno: University of Nevada Oral History Project, 1978-1980), 9-11.

6

Golden Arrow

During the next four years, Longstreet continued to live at Red Rock Ranch in a sometime way, pursuing the mining excitements of the Kawich region with the feverish enthusiasm of a young man who had all the world before him. The winter of 1904–1905 found him in Gold Reed, where O. K. Reed and other prospectors had made a strike. The *Tonopah Bonanza* enthusiastically reported "a chunk of ore twice as large as a man's head which is literally alive with gold" and an outcropping from which free gold was visible at a distance of ten feet.

These discoveries were soon accompanied by rumors of trouble in the Kawich, in the shape of a newspaper story that Longstreet and three others had been killed and several wounded in a grand battle for the possession of a prime mining claim. Later reports moved the scene of the gunfight to Red Rock Ranch, reduced the fatalities to Longstreet and one companion, and shifted the cause to an altercation with one of the Nays over the price of hay. The friends and relatives of those involved remained "naturally somewhat distrubed," so a deputy sheriff was dispatched "after the prisoners and the dead."

Longstreet must have had a good laugh when the law officer arrived to examine his carcass. Though the story was swiftly contradicted, there may have been a kernel of truth hidden inside like the sweet bean within the mesquite husk that Longstreet's squaw had mashed into meal on her Ash Meadows grinding stone.

Longstreet also made an appearance at another new mining camp in the Kawich christened Silverbow and located
near the former Breen ranch. Here he staked a claim to the
Southern Belle in the summer of 1905, and it is not unlikely
that his proficiency with a Colt .44 enabled him to take and
hold his ground. Claim jumping was acknowledged to be rife
in Silverbow. And who would be better qualified to partici-
pate in such affrays than the man who was both a veteran of
the Chispa and possibly the best shot west of the Utah
border? Enough is known of Longstreet's ways to make a
pretty good guess.

Despite the perils of joining the rush to the new strikes in
the Kawich, the Gold Reed ore sample placed on display in
the window of the Nye County Bank in Tonopah, together
with reported assays of $50 to $800 a ton, created a sensation
that few prospectors could ignore. In the words of the *Bonanza*, "Every available team in the camp was soon pressed
into service and the stampede to the new district began in
earnest." These ardent spirits were not destined to find all
the comforts of home. "Kawich is a hell of a place! No mines,
no water, no feed, no women," an early visitor reported. The
Bonanza warned eager prospectors "not to depend" on finding water out in the Kawich. None at all could be obtained at
Gold Reed, the nearest source being a small trickle at Antelope Springs fifteen miles away.

As these sharp warnings stressed, not every man could
survive in the Kawich, not even under the fairly temperate
conditions of winter. On a hot day in the desert—and
summer brings a good many such days—the human body
can lose as much as a quart of moisture in an hour through
perspiration, unnoticed because it immediately evaporates;
someone engaged in strenuous activity needs at least two
gallons of water per day, or he will slowly dehydrate,
weaken, and die. As loss of water thickens his blood, his
heart labors, his head aches, and his limbs grow weary. Dizz-
iness, stumbling footsteps, and blurred speech soon follow.

The final stages of dehydration are inaugurated by delirium, muscle spasms, and a swollen tongue. When the victim collapses in the sands for the last time, scarcely able to see or hear, bloody fissures appear in his shriveled skin before he dies.

By 1905 death and dementia in the desert were sharply on the rise, as heedless fortune hunters seized with Goldfield and Bullfrog fever fanned out into a region still only partially mapped. In Death Valley alone heat and thirst claimed at least thirteen lives that summer, and one newspaper report placed the toll as high as thirty-five. The California legislature was the first to pass an appropriation for desert signposts to reduce the number of those who died lost in the desert, sometimes never knowing that water was close at hand. The problem was, if anything, more acute in Nevada, where more than a million acres of the desert between Lida, Ash Meadows, and the Kawich had not yet been mapped by section lines and the U.S. government was being petitioned to begin a complete survey of the area.

In the summer of 1905, spurred by three more deaths and another crazed man led into town by travelers, the Tonopah and Goldfield newspapers agitated for action: "No time should be lost, for the heat in that desolate region is intense and, in fact, unbearable at this time of the year, and a few guideposts may be the means of saving the lives of many prospectors." The Nye County Board of Commissioners responded by appointing Jack Longstreet to signpost the desert south and east of Tonopah. The commissioners' choice was singularly appropriate: what hand should better mark this last frontier for the lesser men to follow than the hard, seamed hand of its last survivor?

By the end of 1907, Gold Reed was a ghost town, and the 600 locations staked during the pandemonium three years earlier had turned back into worthless sand. But there were other places for Longstreet: placer claims thirteen miles west of Duckwater, the strike in the Monitor range that was to preoccupy the last years of his life, and, in the Golden Arrow district, the stillborn camp of Longstreet, named in his honor by Claude and Marl Page, two young deaf-mute Missouri-born prospectors whom he had befriended.

No messenger was more welcome than Longstreet when he rode into Tonopah with news of more discoveries at the Golden Arrow site beside the domed hill on the edge of the Kawich. The assays on the gold and silver in Longstreet's own portion of the ground came in so high that even he expressed surprise. For a few exhilarating days in February, it seemed that the long-sought bonanza was finally in reach, and a tent city briefly flowered at Golden Arrow, culminating during 1907 in a wooden hotel, several saloons, and a mill with ten stamps, descending pestles that crushed ore more efficiently than the old arrastra method. Erratic efforts at development over the next several years were followed by the usual collapse. Though the Pages reportedly sold their claims for a handsome price, the town they had so hopefully platted in the winter of 1905–1906 was never built, and the name that stuck was that of the district, Golden Arrow. The camp of Longstreet, which had no more substantial existence than the trembling, watery pavilions of a mirage, no longer even appears on the maps.

While the story that Longstreet was involved in the stampede to Arrowhead in the next range across the valley east of the Kawich can not be substantiated, it is true that it was unlike him to sit out a rush. You could ride so late that the gray, ghostly owls flapped up from the pale sagebrush, startled in their midnight hunting; you could start so early that the dry grass was a glinting gold web in the first light while darkness lingered on the mountains. But when you arrived at the new strike, Longstreet would probably be there before you, his big, bearded, long-haired figure crouching by the campfire with a rifle resting lightly across his knees. And you would not catch him unawares. Glasscock relates, "Whenever he saw a traveler in the desert he would dismount from his horse, unlimber his gun and stand on the far side of the animal until the traveler disappeared or came near enough to be recognized." Glasscock considers that precautions such as these had enabled Longstreet to survive so long:

> It is of record that on one occasion in Stone Cabin Valley the travelers who had stirred his suspicion cut down on him with their rifles. Longstreet tied his horse's bridle to one ankle to leave his hands free for the use of his guns, and crawled to partial cover in the sage-brush. Evidently he considered it good tactics to keep the horse within reach for possible escape, even if the animal threatened to disturb his aim. And with the horse dancing in fright at the whining bullets and crashing six-guns, Jack Longstreet fought off his attackers.

An even wilder narrative of Longstreet's prowess with his gun in this period was related by Andy McAllister, an early miner in Goldfield. Just what proportions of gospel truth and tall tale went into it will ever remain a secret known only to the teller. According to newspaperman Elton Garrett, to whom McAllister told the story, he and Longstreet were deer hunting in the mountains between Red Rock Ranch and Silverbow. The date was probably 1904, when a newspaper report placed McAllister as well as Longstreet in the Kawich. Although Longstreet was usually so taciturn where his past was concerned that even his closest friends knew very little about him, something about the feel of the hunt and the warm sun slanting through the pinon and juniper put him in a reminiscent mood. He began telling McAllister about the deer hunts of other years. As the two followed the rocky trail higher into the mountains, Longstreet drifted off from recollections of long-ago deer hunts into stories of his "manhunt-

ing exploits." Soon McAllister was listening in utter amaze-
ment to "such tales of desert battling and bloodshed as he
never had heard before."

The two deer hunters eventually decided to separate. Still
hoping for a buck apiece, they planned to skirt opposite rims
of the hill looming before them and meet in the saddle on the
far side. When McAllister reached the appointed spot an
hour later, Longstreet was not yet in sight. Wearily, McAllister lay down to wait and began to doze in the late afternoon
sun. The blood-chilling stories he had just heard were still
curling through his imagination, and "dreams of men being
drawn and quartered and then shot full of rock salt by Jack
Longstreet commenced stumbling through his brain."

He was awakened by the crack of a bullet beside his head.
Leaping to his feet, he saw Longstreet standing nearby with
a smoking gun. McAllister did not pause to ask questions.
Instead he sprinted down the mountainside "like a startled
deer."

Longstreet started after him. No! This was no dream!
There came the desert man behind him as fast as he could
pelt.

Andy doubled his speed down the slope, visions of may-
hem and murder still racing through his cranium. Had
Longstreet gone mad? What could be the matter. It was
preposterous! Yet there was Longstreet, pursuing him, yel-
ling at him to stop.

Well, he wouldn't stop! Not by a long shot. He ran ducking from side to side to dodge possible bullets. Mile after
mile he put behind him, until he had left Jack Longstreet
far behind.

McAllister claimed that he did not pause in his flight until
he had put seventy miles of distance, "more or less," between
himself and Longstreet. They did not again encounter each
other for some time; McAllister made sure of that. When he
eventually ran into the familiar tall, long-haired figure,

McAllister was poised for another hasty retreat, but Longstreet's demeanor appeared friendly.

"Hey, you didn't need to be so scared that time," he drawled. "I got him the first shot."

"Got who the first shot?" asked McAllister.

"The rattler. He was coiled near your head, and I knew if I got too close he'd strike you. So I blasted away!"

At about the time of this memorable deer hunt in the Kawich, after years of ducking when the lightning struck, Longstreet became a well-to-do man by the standards of the period. On March 2, 1906, he sold Red Rock Ranch for $5,000 to Captain W. G. Cotter, a mining man who had also purchased numerous mining claims from him in the course of the preceding year. His cattle were sold too, reputedly to the Reeds, who ranched on the broad stretches of Cactus Flat west of the mountains and were friendly with Longstreet. These cattle of Longstreet's had thrived in summer on the secret patches of meadowland hidden around the Bellehelen Lakes high in the Kawich, and in winter on the dried, pale-gold Indian ricegrass that quilted the lower slopes. They had grown in their seasonal wanderings, with minimal husbandry by Longstreet, to a large and valuable herd.

More profits floated into Longstreet's hands through dealings in Greenwater, a short-lived copper camp in the Black Mountains east of Death Valley; his partners in this and various other mining schemes were Frank McAllister and Wake Catlett, the latter a Kentuckian and another of the Southern friends with whom Longstreet seemed to find a particular affinity. When Rhyolite Judge L. O. Ray and others hatched a scheme to pipe water to thirsty Greenwater from Ash Meadows, Longstreet sold them his Ash Meadows property for a reported $10,000 on September 6, 1906.

Judge Ray no doubt thought it well worth the money. Water in booming Greenwater never cost less than ten cents a gallon. Teams hauling the scarce commodity consumed half of all they carried just to last the round trip. The editors of the *Greenwater Miner* and the *Death Valley Chuck-Walla* considered it cheaper to let their newspaper plant burn to the ground than to extinguish a fire with Greenwater's high-priced water. After persuading investors from as far away as South Africa to help finance his $1,500,000 scheme, Ray announced grandiose plans: a pumping station in Ash Meadows, ninety miles of water mains, and a master reservoir in the Funeral Mountains to supply Greenwater and several other Death Valley camps, fed by the pulsing aquamarine pools where Longstreet had watered his horses for a time, and then moved on.

It was the critical moment to sell. The eastern financier Charles Schwab himself, who made a fortune at Greenwater at considerable cost to more gullible investors and to his own reputation, could not have timed it better. By the summer of 1907, the Greenwater bubble had burst, leaving the pipeline scheme literally high and dry and the claims nearly worthless. The mining excitements in the Kawich, which had briefly escalated the value of Longstreet's water rights at Red Rock Ranch, were not destined to last much longer. Regardless, Longstreet was believed to have made in the vicinity of $30,000, a considerable change for someone who little more than a decade before had been unable to scrape together a few dollars in taxes for the Oasis Valley ranch, someone who had stayed locked in the Belmont jail for weeks, unable to pay his fine.

So, the man who laconically observed that he had neglected to uncover the riches of the Hackberry mine and El Dorado Canyon due to "too much whiskey," the man who sometimes may have reflected that had he done a little more prospecting in the vicinity of his Oasis Valley spread he might have happened on the spot where the treasure trove of the future Montgomery-Shoshone mine lay waiting to be discovered, tumbled into riches in spite of himself.

It did not change his way of life at all. To most of the men

Longstreet's long-time friend and business associate Orville K. Reed (left), with Harry Lorigan (Nevada Historical Society)

around him, new-found wealth meant erecting a fine, substantial house, buying a prime ranch, opening a store or a saloon, investing in solid stocks, endowing a church or a new building for their fraternal lodge, or having a grand fling in San Francisco, perhaps even Europe. At the very least, a man of more than sixty years was apt to see a great deal of money as a means of taking his ease.

Longstreet did none of these things. The grand fling was out of the question for a man with a severed ear. Instead he had his flings in riotous drinking bouts and hours spent gambling while seated with crossed legs around the blanket with his old Indian friends in Ash Meadows, where none would look askance at the scarred place concealed beneath his long hair. They were his lodge. His church, if he had one, was the far country, maybe the smoke-stained caves of the Ancient Ones. The prosperous stores and saloons, the fine ranches, were for the builders who wanted to parlay their investments into ever greater fortunes. He cared for none of that. He had run his shabby little down-at-the-heels stores and his tent saloons as a way of coming into the country, taking, as the trapper does, no more than he needs to live. He had wanted his impecunious ranches so the horses would have a grazing place, and he left them, as he left the Moapa place, when they showed signs of consuming him. He had staked his mining claims less for the hope of gain than for the electric charge of being part of the stampede, the dark thrill of pitting his steel against the rest when he fought for his ground. It was the greatest race of all, and he had always loved a race.

Now he worked as a shotgun guard on the Tonopah stage, though he was actually a good deal richer than most of the passengers he guarded. Distrusting banks—with good reason, as the disastrous Nevada bank failures of 1907 were to show—he often carried his money around with him in an old suitcase. He bought or traded a few small mining claims, always out on the fringe. And he allowed himself one grand, luxurious indulgence, the purchase of a few fine thoroughbred horses. These are said to have been shipped all the way from Kentucky, though it is not known if they raced so well for him as the Indian pony of long ago.

The Kentucky horses would be needing a pasture, so once more Longstreet turned north.

Notes

Longstreet's involvement in the mining excitements at Gold Reed, Golden Arrow, Arrowhead, and the Monitor range is derived from the *Tonopah Bonanza*, December 31, 1904, January 7, 1905, February 17 and 23, 1906, and November 1–2, 1907; the *Goldfield*

Daily Tribune, July 16, 1907; the *Tonopah Miner*, July 27, 1907; Glasscock, *Gold in Them Hills*, 212-16; his obituary in the *Tonopah Mining Reporter*, July 28, 1928; and mining records in the Nye County courthouse. Paher summarizes the history of these districts in *Nevada Ghost Towns and Mining Camps*, 332, 345-46; and the Longstreet townsite receives mention in the *Goldfield Review*, February 8, 1906, and the *Goldfield News*, February 16, 1906. Further details on the reported gunfight in the Kawich appear in the *Tonopah Miner*, January 7, 1905. On Greenwater, see L. Burr Belden, *Mines of Death Valley*, (Glendale, Calif.: La Siesta Press, 1976), 34-37, and Glasscock, *Gold in Them Hills*, 264-86. For the story of the Ash Meadows Water Company, see the *Goldfield Weekly News*, January 26, April 27, and June 1, 1907, and the *Goldfield Daily Tribune*, June 13, 1907.

Longstreet's appointment to signpost the desert is reported in the *Goldfield Review*, August 31, 1905, with recent deaths in the desert appearing in the August 10 issue and in Lingenfelter, *Death Valley & the Amargosa*, 13; also see the *Tonopah Bonanza*, July 22, 1905; human physiology under desert conditions is discussed in A. Starker Leopold, *The Desert* (New York: Time-Life Books, 1969), 127-29. McAllister's story appears in Elton Garrett, "Nuggets of Nevada Color," *Tonopah, Nevada, Mining Record-Reporter*, April 25, 1931.

7

McCann Pass

North of Red Rock Ranch, Cactus Flat merges imperceptibly into the Stone Cabin Valley. The Kawich sinks like an old stag run to ground and is reborn as the Hot Creek range. The Monitor Hills, which seem to drown on the western horizon beneath the heavy sand and pale green brush of the flat, struggle free and rise high, and higher still, to the heights of the Monitor range.

In the spring of 1906, soon after the sale of Red Rock Ranch, Longstreet packed his few belongings in his wagon, laid his rifle in its usual place beside him on the seat, and headed north into these mountains. He passed the Clifford place at Stone Cabin, not minding that he would be living nearer the enemy now and he would have to run the gantlet of the Clifford guns every time he went to town. His teams clopped steadily onward, past mesas that washed out into the valley from the Monitor in long, smooth mulberry-colored waves. He passed the springs where the cowboys heading north paused to water their herds, Fourmile Spring, Side Hill Spring, Point of Rock Spring, Warm Spring. He had sold that many springs and more to Cotter along with Red Rock Ranch: Mule Spring, Willow, Hillside, Gravel, Collar, Cottonwood, Meadow, Mud, Canon. Cotter had wanted every trickle spelled out in the deed.

So indifferent had Longstreet grown to ranching that he

did not bother to homestead more than forty acres. He was done with running the big herds, unconcerned with the value of the place, having already more money in the old suitcase tossed behind him in the wagon than he knew how to spend. No matter that a little forty-acre ranch with a single good spring was worthless to anyone but him. He had what he wanted, a secret hideaway locked deep inside a canyon, with enough cover for a man to defend himself against an army if he had to, enough pasture for the horses, an apple tree hardy enough to survive at 7,000 feet, a little stable, a blacksmith shop, and a corral of cedar fencing, built circular and angled outward for breaking horses. In the sagebrush on the north side of the canyon, across from the clear stream, through thickets of wild rose entwined with red columbine, he dug his root cellar. A few feet from the stable in the clearing he built a small cabin of logs chinked with mud, stretched canvas tightly over the roof, brought in his stove, his old metal steamer trunk, and his iron bedstead. It was fortunate, as it turned out, that he had a place for the new woman.

The year in which Fannie Black Longstreet became "Jack's squaw," as she was to be known for the rest of her life, remains a matter of debate. She was an Ash Meadows Southern Paiute, probably from the mixed Paiute and Shoshone band called the Kauyaichits, and there is no doubt that Longstreet must have known her while living there, as well as her sinister brother Bob and her sister, the wife of Longstreet's close friend Albert Howell. Some believe that she had been Jack's woman since the 1890s and that the white petticoats hoisted aloft to announce the surrender at the Chispa were hers. Yet a few old-timers remember stories of another Indian wife after the move to the Kawich, which is to some degree confirmed by the presence of another name, Susie Longstreet, a Paiute completely surrounded by Shoshone, on the 1900 census in the same precinct with Longstreet's. Glasscock, who knew them for years, related that

Fannie became Longstreet's woman in Rhyolite and gave enough detail to suggest that he might have known what he was talking about.

If it happened in Rhyolite, the date was no earlier than the camp's discovery in 1905, and more likely in 1906. By then, Rhyolite was a booming city of imposing stone edifices, built to last forever and destined soon for ruin, its streets thronged with crowds and wandering burros, its sky pallid with heat over mountains crusted with black rock or slashed with ruddy, slanting striations. Fannie had taken up with a gambler of vicious temperament, with whom she was living in Rhyolite.

With his Greenwater interests, the deal with Judge Ray pending, and his recurrent need for a few days of roistering with the Ash Meadows crowd, Longstreet had plenty of good reasons for a journey south just then. Providentially for Fannie, he camped on Rhyolite's outskirts to have a look around the new boomtown. Perhaps she saw the familiar tall, long-haired figure striding through the dusty throng at a distance or crossing the threshold at the Southern Hotel (he would have applauded the name) for a thirst-quencher; perhaps a word or more had passed between them.

At any rate, when her lover beat her, it was to Longstreet that she fled for protection, and she was not disappointed. The gambler followed with gun in hand, hard on her heels, to reclaim her. If he considered that a man was entitled to beat his squaw when he felt like it, if he thought it taught her the proper respect, especially a woman like this one, with such a gay, pleasant tongue that white folks kept forgetting and treating her as if she were almost as good as themselves, if he figured that his main mistake was not whaling her hard enough, there were not too many men in Rhyolite in 1906 who would have been disposed to dispute him on any of these points.

It was his ill luck to encounter one of the few who would. The approaching gambler was met by a pair of blue eyes that glittered like sun glancing off glass in the sand. A stranger would have guessed that Longstreet was then in his fifties, rather than nearly seventy, yet would draw little comfort from the grayness in his beard and his long hair. Longstreet had aged in the way of a well-worn bull whip that has been around long enough to grow supple and get the quirks cracked out. Whatever it was that passed through the gambler's mind as he confronted those glittering blue eyes, it dissuaded him from using his gun. Longstreet knocked him into the dust, which in view of the usual Longstreet preference for guns sounds a good deal like a blow for a blow, a taste of the man's own medicine in the feel of a hard fist smashing into the flesh. In Glasscock's phrase, "Fanny was Jack's squaw thereafter." And Fannie knew how to be grateful.

So it was that when Longstreet finished his business and turned the wagon north, she sat beside him on the seat, her long black hair braided down her back, her brown, full-lipped face with the high cheekbones quick and alert, the frowning brow, characteristic of her people, concealing the warm, gay spirit within, as her long, loose-fitting dress concealed the slender, graceful figure inside. She was then about forty years old, as nearly as she could reckon such things, born when Longstreet was already a grown man following his hidden path west. She had been schooled in the ancient ways of her people in a time when the white man was no more than distant thunder on the Indian horizon. Then, during the terrible fifteen years after 1890, she had seen almost two of every three Indians in her corner of the world die from sicknesses of body and spirit that the census taker ascribed to the white man's whiskey and his love. She had lived on, as much a survivor in her way as Longstreet.

At night she made camp, as she was to do on their journeyings for more than twenty years, unharnessing the horses, cooking their supper, and preparing their bedrolls, while Longstreet lazed around in the time-honored way of the In-

The sling on Longstreet's arm suggests that this photo with Fannie was the last one taken before his death (Nevada Historical Society)

dian warrior who is lord to his woman. Sometimes he watched her, so ceaselessly busy to please him. And she did please him, very well indeed. By day they traveled on, a man and a woman in an old buckboard moving slowly north across the vast desert under a vaster sky.

The trouble was that, in taking Fannie, Longstreet soon found he had also taken her brother Bob Black. He had, of course, known Black for years. Black was part of that secret Ash Meadows world that few white men other than Longstreet would ever know. It was a world of hideous revenge where an Indian named Crazy Henry had pulled out the fingernails of his unfaithful squaw with a pair of pliers, setting off a terrible blood feud that decimated entire families.

It was a world, too, of sudden, mysterious deaths, later recounted with the invariable caveat, "Of course, there was a lot of killing in those days, and people didn't think much about it." They told of the man who sang, "Eat, drink, and be merry, for tomorrow you may die," in a Beatty saloon and was shot within the hour, the grim sort of joke that brings a flickering smile in Ash Meadows. When the body of a man with a rope twisted around his neck was found out in the low sagebrush by a dry lake, law officers called it "accidental death." A local said it was "the first man I ever knowed what hung hisself laying on the ground"—cause for another grim smile.

Sometimes the perpetrators of these deeds were briefly called north to answer for them, but more often not. As long-time Ash Meadows resident George Ishmael has said of one of these murderers, "They just let him stay around, no more than if he was shooting a dog." Even the ceremonies of the region retained an aura of grisly cruelty. On the death of Chief Tecopa in 1905, the Indians raced all his horses until they could run no farther, then shot the staggering animals and set all the chief's belongings in flames on the traditional Southern Paiute funeral pyre.

Of all the desperadoes in this ruthless world, none was more feared than Bob Black, Fannie's renegade brother. Spokane prospector Fred Birney later related that when he stopped at Ash Meadows with his partner Phil Creasor in January 1905, Black had told him in broken English of the unexplored Greenwater region. Actually, claims had already been located in the area, as Black may have been well aware when he enticed Birney and Creasor into the farther hills with his alluring tales of a rich mining country known only to the Indians. Soon after the pair headed out with their burros toward their imminent discovery at Greenwater, Black embarked upon a murderous binge in which he killed at least four people, including his squaw, his brother, and two other men. Although Birney and Creasor did not realize it, the bloody debauch in Ash Meadows may have occupied the Indian long enough to save them from shallow graves in the sandy wasteland. Not all travelers had fared so well. The remains of murdered prospectors found in the desert from time to time mutely testified that the dry spring and the fierce sun were not the only menaces to human life in the Death Valley region. Dead men told no tales, but these killings were widely believed to be the work of Bob Black.

If the unidentified bodies gnawed by predators and desiccated by the heat were indeed Black's victims, it is not clear whether they were slain for their race, their meager possessions, or their prospecting activities. He himself was a prospector of some ability, credited with more than the doubtful distinction of contributing to the Greenwater strike. The rich ledges uncovered south of Ivanpah at Vanderbilt in 1891 were Black's discovery, although he received virtually nothing for his pains. Four years later when his cousin Mary Scott showed him some gold float she had found on a hunting trip near the old Ibex mine in the Black Mountains on the east side of Death Valley, Black prevailed upon her to show him the spot. It proved to be a promising one, a massive quartz ledge with pockets of gold that later assayed as high as $250 a ton. Once the secret of Mary's gold was his, Black demonstrated that he could take advantage of an Indian kinswoman as quickly as the white men had cheated him at Vanderbilt. He is said to have recompensed Mary Scott for her kindness with twelve bottles of desert wine and sold the site of the Confidence mine to Frank Cole, millwright at the Johnnie, and James Ashdown for $4,000, with which he hoped to purchase Longstreet's Ash Meadows ranch and his herd of horses. George Montgomery then bought into the claim and engineered its sale to the Salt Lake City owners of the Chispa and the Johnnie for $81,000.

Montgomery worked like a whirlwind at developing the Confidence during the winter of 1895-1896. A crew of miners set to work on the ledge, a roller quartz mill and other expensive pieces of equipment were hauled in, and construction began on a road. The returns from the refractory ores at the Confidence nonetheless proved disappointingly paltry. By spring the mine was being dubbed the "Lost Confidence." The Salt Lake investors refused any further expenditures, the work force departed unable to collect their pay, and thousands of dollars in unpaid debts accumulated against the Confidence Mining Company. These obligations included the $4,000 note still owed to Bob Black, though George Montgomery attempted to bank the fires of the Indian's murderous temper by allowing him to draw supplies from the company store without charge.

During the summer of 1896, the Salt Lake City investors dispatched a new superintendent, Thomas Gillespie, to devise more profitable methods of working the ores at the Confidence, the Johnnie, and the Chispa. In an apparent effort to institute more businesslike procedures, Gillespie decreed that Black was to receive nothing further from the company store unless he paid for it. As historian Richard Lingenfelter has recently observed, "It seems to have been a fatal decision." In October Gillespie was fatally shot through the head by an unseen gunman. Although the murderer was never identified, suspicion centered upon Bob Black, whose grudge against Gillespie was well known.

On balance, Mary Scott had probably received greater satisfaction from her twelve bottles of desert wine than did Bob Black from the $4,000 note endorsed to Longstreet but never paid. Now the grassy fields that had been Indian land in the time of his fathers would never belong to Black. The large profits received by Montgomery and the others for the sale of the Confidence may well have fueled the Indian's hatred for white men who reaped the rewards denied to him.

The Confidence mine episode was not the last of Black's prospecting or his bushwhacking. According to author William Caruthers, Black also found some rich float while hunting mountain sheep in the Avawatz Mountains. "Death Valley Scotty" (Walter Scott), who was eager to inject some substance into the myth he was circulating about his fabulous secret mine, accompanied Black on several attempts to locate the ledge where the Indian's chunk of nearly pure gold had originated. Although a cloudburst had set off a flash flood that rearranged the countryside, they succeeded in finding the corners where the Indian had pitched his tent, and Black remained confident that a bonanza ledge would soon be uncovered nearby. Another source recounts that during this period Scotty hired Black as his bodyguard for protection against an unseen sharpshooter who was trying to ambush him. In time, Scotty developed a suspicion that the mysterious bushwhacker and his Indian bodyguard were one and the same man. Probably Scotty's relief when the threat of arrest forced Black to take flight considerably outweighed his regret that the gold in the Avawatz was forever lost to him.

In the aftermath of his January 1905 orgy of drunken murder, Black was compelled to concentrate on his own concealment for several months, though an occasional sign appeared that hinted at his passing. A pack of coyotes gathered near Echo Canyon on the north side of the Funerals led to discovery of the partially buried bodies of three more murdered prospectors in late June. Soon afterward the Indians learned of the renegade's hiding place.

Although they usually preferred to deal with Indian criminals according to tribal custom without interference from white legal authorities, Indian representatives arrived in Goldfield in the summer of 1905 begging lawmen to come after Bob Black so that he could kill no more. The *Goldfield Review* declared that he would "undoubtedly" be taken into custody soon, but law officers showed no greater enthusiasm for the enterprise than was displayed on the earlier occasion of the manhunt for Jim Boone. No arrest was made, nor even seriously attempted. Black stayed on the dodge, his big, powerful figure a shadowy presence glimpsed at twilight like one possessed by the Un-nu-pits, the evil spirits of Indian legend.

This, then, was Fannie's dowry. When she asked him, Longstreet could not refuse sanctuary to her close kinsman, and Black came north to hide at Longstreet's ranch. Trying to make the best of it, Longstreet let Black know he could make himself useful around the place with the smithy and the stock. Longstreet still kept a handful of cattle, fifteen or so, in addition to the horses. They also went prospecting together, and Longstreet came to believe that the ore Black struck at Longstreet Canyon, one canyon south of the cabin in the Monitor, was good enough to work.

For a number of years they got along as well as two very dangerous men could be expected to do, with Fannie there to ease a silence stretched taut or gentle down a hard-edged word. Even if neither one slept too deeply at night, a precarious balance must have developed between them, each knowing the other's measure.

Finally, late in the summer of 1910 during the Indian Moon of Fall Warnings, the breaking point arrived, as it was bound to do, at a moment when Fannie was not there to smooth the quarrel that had been building between them for several months. They had gone to Belmont to buy some machinery from an old mill for the mine and to procure enough supplies for the next two or three months. After the purchases were made and the wagon loaded, Longstreet and Black found time for more than a few drinks, both getting well liquored up. Black's mood had turned ugly and quarrelsome by the time they finally started for home in the lengthening shadows of evening, accompanied by Frank McAllister.

This third member of the party was a former prospector from Ballarat in the Panamints west of Death Valley who had located claims at Greenwater in 1898 and later relocated them in 1904. Longstreet was said to have been profitably involved in McAllister's Greenwater venture, and when McAllister's holdings were sold to Harry Ramsey, Longstreet might not have objected to gleaning some coin from his old adversary in the battle at the Chispa. If so, Longstreet's gains probably stayed crammed in his old suitcase a good deal longer than McAllister's stayed with him. Three years after the sudden demise of the great copper craze, the former Ballarat prospector was apparently down on his luck again and working for Longstreet, who may have been the only employer in the region who felt equal to handling McAllister in one of his gun-happy moods.

Some time after midnight Longstreet decided to make camp near McCann's Summit in the Monitor range. They had not reached the lush, green meadows on the eastern side, but they had covered several miles on a road ascending through steep slopes of broken scree. As the wagons creaked to a halt, McAllister could tell that Black was still feeling his liquor and bent on trouble. Longstreet seemed more restrained, sobered enough by the night ride through the mountains in the cool air to be reminded that this man was his brother-in-law. Had Black been a stranger, Longstreet would long since have dropped for cover and reached for his gun. As it was, Longstreet tried to pacify him.

McAllister set off through the pinon and juniper to tether the mules some distance away. Presently he heard the sound of a scuffle and knew they had come to blows. When Longstreet's voice called out to him for help, McAllister, though prone to brandish his gun in less perilous circumstances, stayed right where he was, busying himself with the mules. Against the backdrop of black mountains falling away on either side as far as the eye could see, he could distinguish their shadowy figures grappling in the darkness. The Indian cried out, "I kill you, Jack Longstreet, you son-of-a-bitch." McAllister heard three shots and saw one figure fall. Longstreet had loosened his arm just enough from Black's grip to reach his gun, squeezing off two bullets into the Indian's legs and one into his abdomen.

Longstreet and McAllister laid the wounded Black in the wagon and brought him back to Belmont. Tom Clifford said years later that Longstreet told him the mortal shot to the

abdomen happened in the wagon. Hearing a sound, Longstreet had turned to see Black digging in his bed roll, apparently after a hidden weapon. Longstreet knew then that
sooner or later he would have to finish him and did the necessary. There is also a floating story that the Indian had found
his concealed gun and attempted to shoot Longstreet
through a knothole in the wagon, but it was the version told
by McAllister, the only witness, that carried the day for
Longstreet.

Black's dying and the legal aftermath were quickly over.
The Indian was cared for in Belmont until Dr. J. C. Garner
arrived later that morning from Manhattan, a nearby mining camp in the green, pinon-wooded folds on the west side of
the Toquima Mountains. Black was then moved to Miners'
Union Hospital in Manhattan, where he died in the late afternoon. Taken into custody by Constable Santos, Longstreet occupied himself with two things. The first was a telephone message to the brilliant young Tonopah lawyer,
future Nevada Attorney General George B. Thatcher, whom
he had evidently chosen as a worthy successor to Key Pittman in the conduct of his legal affairs. Though deeply involved in the final days of a hard-fought primary campaign,
Thatcher presently arrived in Manhattan by auto. A coroner's inquest was held in Manhattan on the evening of Black's
death, Saturday, August 27. Local opinion was already favorable to Longstreet, despite the fact that he had shielded
Black from justice for years. When McAllister told his story
and the jurors were reminded that Black was the renegade
killer wanted for the Ash Meadows murders, the jury lost no
time in deciding that Longstreet had acted in self-defense,
and he was set free. Thatcher soon took care of the rest.

The second order of business was a lavish funeral for Bob
Black. In the belief that Black's evil spirit would return to
harm those who took part in the burial, the Indians refused to
have anything to do with it. It seemed that Bob Black in death
was scarcely less frightening to them than he had been in

life. Whether spurred by unseemly relief at his own liberation
from that evil spirit, by a sharp sense of guilt, or by a desire to
placate Fannie, Longstreet ordered the fine polished wood
coffin, the flowers, and all the best that Manhattan could
offer to give the renegade a funeral worthy of a chief.

Fannie was not so easily placated. Glasscock relates that
she left him. For three weeks the cabin in Windy Canyon remained empty of her presence. In the Glasscock version, it
was hunger that finally brought her back, but it was probably something a good deal stronger than that. Fannie was a
Southern Paiute, daughter of a people trained early to live on
nothingness, to whom the hawks are chickens and the grass
seeds are bread. The day had probably never dawned when
hunger would drive her like a dog to whine at the heels of the
man who would feed her.

Her going probably had more to do with the rites of mourn-
ing and the blood feuds that run deep and hidden in the Ash
Meadows country as the Amargosa River flows invisible
under the sand. Maybe it even had to do with grief for the
brother who, in a time when so many of the tribe had sick-
ened and fallen like yellow leaves, had fought back in dark
fury at all that offended him and turned himself into an
avenger who stalked the hills and served the prospectors'
greed with death. In the older, better times, given warrior
enemies, her brother might have been a hero whose deeds in
war would long have been sung around the campfires after
he was gone, instead of a renegade with the knife point of his
anger slashing suicidally inward upon his own people.

The autumn nights were already frosty, the aspens rustled
gold, and the chokecherries had ripened into bitter fruit by
the time Fannie returned to the cabin in Windy Canyon.
Longstreet is said to have accepted her in silence, and some
remember a strange kind of constraint between them, almost
as though the man who had faced every danger of the frontier had come to fear his woman. She served him once more,
in the old way, but Bob Black's death sifted between them as

fog fills the Stone Cabin Valley the morning after a thunder-storm, isolating every mountain as a dark island onto itself. Perhaps the Indians who refused to take part in the burial had foreseen more than Longstreet was ready to believe when he dismissed their superstitious warnings. Bob Black had not stayed in his fine, fancy coffin after all. He had re-turned, as the Indians had known he would, in the still hoot of the owl at midnight in which the voices of the unquiet dead speak again, in the twisting face remembered from a troubled dream in which Ghost Man comes to demand his due from the living, and in the coldness that had formed like an ice cave in the depths of Fannie's black eyes.

Notes

For the story of Longstreet and Fannie Black, see Glasscock, *Gold in Them Hills*, 214-15; a different version appears in Lewis, "Jack Longstreet." Additional details on Fannie, her brother, and the Longstreet ranch were drawn from Longstreet's probate records. The estimate on the decimation of the local Indian population is that of census taker Harsha White, who also recounted the funeral of Chief Tecopa (*Goldfield Review*, September 28, 1905). Material on Frank McAllister appears in Lingenfelter, *Death Valley & the Amargosa*, 313-14, 317. On squaw men, see Colin G. Calloway, "Neither White nor Red: White Renegades on the American Indian Frontier," *Western Historical Quarterly* 17 (January 1986): 46-54, and Bil Gilbert, *Westering Man: The Life of Joseph Walker* (New York: Atheneum, 1983), 41-44, 161-71.

Sources on Bob Black were the *Manhattan Mail*, August 27, 1910; the *Goldfield Daily News*, August 30, 1910; the *Carson City News*, August 31, 1910; the *Nevada State Journal*, September 8, 1910; Longstreet's obituary in the *Tonopah Mining Reporter*, July 28, 1928; the *Goldfield Review*, July 13, 1905; the *Inyo Register*, De-cember 7, 1906; Caruthers, *Loafing along Death Valley Trails*, 90-91, 132; Lingenfelter, *Death Valley & the Amargosa*, 192-94, and Coolidge, *Death Valley Prospectors*, 165-66. Like many stories connected with the con man Walter Scott, Coolidge's should be viewed with some skepticism. William R. Palmer discusses Indian beliefs in *Pahute Indian Legends* (Salt Lake City: Deseret Book Publishers, 1946). This chapter drew on the oral recollections of Sonia De Hart (August 1981), Alice Lorigan, George Ishmael, and Joseph Clifford.

8
Windy Canyon

When the snows retreated toward the mountain peaks, it was time for Longstreet to set out on his annual search for the Lost Breyfogle gold, the elusive phantom that had fired the imagination of Western prospectors for more than half a century.

Longstreet claimed he had known Charles Breyfogle well, which raises some interesting questions. Both men had prospected in the Hualapai, as well as southern Nevada, but Breyfogle was last heard of near Austin in 1869 and Longstreet does not appear in the southern country until 1880—at least, not under that name. It is also possible that Longstreet knew Breyfogle only at second hand from the accounts of William Stockton, the dedicated hunter of lost mines he had known in Oasis Valley, and of the Ash Meadows Indians who had attacked and nearly killed the hulking prospector because they coveted his impressively large shoes.

In fact, Longstreet hinted at the last of these possibilities. He said that in addition to the tip received from Breyfogle himself he relied on information supplied to him by Indians "familiar with the circumstances that attended the killing of Breyfogle," as the Carson City *Appeal* tactfully phrased it. The Indians may indeed have known more about the matter than they were likely to admit to any white man but Longstreet. Although Breyfogle's death remains shrouded in mystery to this day, his relatives believe that he succumbed to blood poisoning after he was shot by an Indian arrow on the way to his lost gold.

The head injury sustained in the earlier encounter with Indians who fancied his shoes no doubt contributed to Breyfogle's downward spiral into madness, and the real story of his prospecting forays into the environs of Death Valley in 1864–1865 may never be unscrambled. But whether his unreliable accounts of his discovery were the maunderings of a deteriorating mind or the cunning obfuscations of a secretive prospector, the valuable bits of ore he carried with him spoke with resounding clarity to many gold seekers. His subsequent attempts to lead prospectors back to the site he had found and lost ended in confusion. He would set out confidently in search of the hill and the mesquite tree that he remembered, then waver and lose his bearings among the myriad hills and mesquite trees of that hallucinatory landscape. One of the parties that he led very nearly killed him in a fury of disappointed greed.

Some prospectors comb the desert even yet, in the belief that a sudden cloudburst buried the Lost Breyfogle and it still lies waiting out there, somewhere. Others are convinced that the lost mine has been rediscovered in Manhattan, Ellendale, Goldfield, and countless other sites scattered as far north as Humboldt County. Probably the spot most frequently mentioned as its true locale is the Johnnie mine near the Chispa on the edge of the Pahrump Valley.

Longstreet, despite his intimate acquaintance with these mines in the course of the gun battle that ended the life of Phil Foote, was not of this persuasion. He placed the site north and west of Death Valley, somewhere in the mountains near Sylvania, where he had run his tent saloon. With how much dedication he had hunted the Lost Breyfogle then, we do not know, possibly not much more vigorously than he had pursued his prospecting in the days when he had overlooked his El Dorados. But the search was all, the discovery far less. He rode out, pointing his horse southwest. At the edge of the rose-colored undulations of the Kawich lay Golden Arrow, moribund in the spring sun; just eight years ago he had spurred his galloping horse to the cities with news of the latest discoveries there. He passed Tonopah and Goldfield, quiet, industrious towns now, drained of the feverish excitement of the old days when he nearly shot Clifford in the Tonopah Mining Company office.

There were different roads to follow from Tonopah. One could head south on the main road from Goldfield to Lida and east to Sylvania. Or take the path he had followed after his release from the Belmont jail, due east to Silver Peak. A little to the south lay Stimler, a scattering of deserted miners' cabins. Hidden deep beneath its tumbled rocks lay the undiscovered treasure that would one day make it a great silver producer. The golden light of late afternoon sifted like dust over a multitude of mysterious canyons like Stimler and the secrets locked inside. Just now, in 1915, Lida was humming again. Murphy, whose cabin the Indians had surrounded after the Ghost Dance, had owned a valuable mining claim there. He had been caught several years later selling whiskey to Indians. Rather than face an inquiry that might progress to stage robberies and other sensitive aspects of his past, Murphy had disappeared, abandoning the mine that would have made him rich in a few years' time. No one knew where he had fled.

Longstreet rode on, through mining camps past and passing and to come. He had seen them born and reborn. Few of them he had not tasted in their rowdiest young days when hope was green enough to fight for; all of them he had fled when solid buildings began to replace the tents, brokers opened offices, and big mining companies bought up the claims, put the men in barracks, and set them working shifts. Time and again he had seen it happen, and every time he had sold out, packed up his woman, when he had one, and ridden on before he could get rich and permanent, heading for a new place where the frontier seemed to be starting all over again.

South of Stimler in the mountains near the Nevada-California border lay wilder country, some of it untouched as the world he had ridden into when he headed west as a young man right after the war. He would stay on there into late May, camping at the shady springs, until the hills turned iridescent with wildflowers, white, blue, purple, and red, and the swift-flying brilliance of birds—blue jays, orioles, and more kinds than a man could name—startled the eye. He was an old man now, but the wild country still made him young. Maybe the Lost Breyfogle was out there, and maybe not. Anyway, in the April sun, with the snow on the Sylvania mountains shrinking to a thin, sugary crust, sharply stippled with black timber, and the high Sierra rising beyond, quilled with shining canyons like the wing of a snowy owl, there was good reason for going.

If old habits stayed, old quarrels died. At least, some of them did. Ellen and Joe Nay had purchased the Barley Creek Ranch north of McCann Pass with their gains from Ellendale, the mining camp that blossomed from Ellen's discovery of a rich pocket of gold near Salisbury Wash. Though his gunshot wound left him stiff-legged and in pain throughout his life, Nay managed to ride horseback and carry on with his ranch work by sheer force of will. He bore no enmity toward Longstreet, who he believed had mistaken him for one of the Cliffords, and the two of them became, in the phrase of Nay's grandson, "the best of friends." While the story that Longstreet was the real discoverer of Ellendale and turned the strike over to the Nays as a kindly gesture is almost certainly false, Longstreet did help to authenticate the claims in the eyes of the public. When serious questions were raised concerning the validity of the Ellendale strike, Longstreet informed the press that he was confident the strike was real because he had once found a piece of rich gold float at the site but never succeeded in tracing its source. He also publicly declared himself "very glad" that Nay had not perished in the gunfight near Red Rock Ranch "for he is not such a bad fellow." Privately, Longstreet is said to have asked and received Nay's forgiveness.

Ellen, on the other hand, forgave him nothing. Her daughter remembered the day when Ellen saw Longstreet's buckboard coming over the hill and remarked to her husband, "Well, Dad, that's Jack Longstreet coming. Now don't you ask him in for dinner!"

"You're going to give him dinner with the rest of them," Nay told her firmly. And Ellen did. She was an excellent cook, but the atmosphere around the table was not conducive to the full enjoyment of her renowned baking powder biscuits, even by a Southerner who knew how to appreciate them. Hostility crackled in every line of Ellen's small, erect body and the tilt of her dark head. The Nays' little girls, Leafy and Emma Nevada, stared in open resentment at the big, long-haired man with the gun who was seated at their table. Leafy remembered that he was "nice enough" but seemed ill at ease. Longstreet did not appear at the Barley Creek Ranch again, though Nay occasionally stopped by the cabin in Windy Canyon for a sociable visit.

After old Ed and Ed Clifford, Jr., died within six weeks of each other in 1916, the atmosphere between Longstreet and the surviving men of the Clifford family perceptibly warmed. Tom Clifford continued to work the ranch in Stone Cabin Valley, and Longstreet got in the habit of stopping by on his trips back to Windy Canyon from Tonopah. Tom's little daughter Marguerite was always happy to see his buckboard coming along the road because she knew he would be bringing a sack of hard candy for her.

On one of these occasions, Longstreet noticed that Tom was having trouble because the mustangs he had rounded up kept breaking out of the corral. Longstreet told him to round them up again. He said he had learned to solve the problem when mustangs got in with his thoroughbred horses and "tried to break."

Tom said, "It's useless. They just keep breaking out."

"I'm telling you, gather them up again," said Longstreet.

Tom did as he was told. Soon the mustangs were roiling around the corral. Again they burst free, but after Longstreet cocked his .44 and dropped two of them, the rest of the horses stayed quietly in the corral.

It was the kind of solution likely to occur to a man who used to shoot buffalo just for the marrow in their bones, considered a choice delicacy by many frontiersmen. Longstreet once remarked that he had worked as a cowboy and a buffalo hunter in Montana. He had been paid $2 a day, forty-five buffalo was his best day's work, and he had found it "great sport."

Now that enough years had passed, Longstreet had grown almost as easy with his former enemy Jim Clifford as he was with Tom. Indeed a strange sort of camaraderie had developed between them, almost as though having nearly killed each other in the gunfight in the Kawich had bonded them together. Jim got so that he could joke about the blood blister where Longstreet's bullet had grazed his face, and Longstreet could jocularly remark of the piece of beard Jim had shot off his jaw, "That's the closest I ever came to dying."

Throughout these years, Longstreet was evolving into something of a local hero. When he rode into Tonopah in March 1907, with news of a strike at Golden Arrow, the *Tonopah Sun* made use of the occasion for political purposes. Longstreet's supposed opinions on the Industrial Workers of the World were featured under the headline, "Hardy Pioneer Is Strongly Opposed to Methods and Work of Agitators." While the threat to send any labor organizers who appeared in Golden Arrow "down the wash" sounds authentic enough, much of the following interview has the ring of *Sun* editor Lindley Branson's fulminations rather than Longstreet. It is primarily of interest because it reveals an attempt by editor Branson to lend greater authority to his newspaper campaign against the radical labor organization by placing words in the mouth of the "hardy pioneer."

In time, nearly any comment from Longstreet was featured in the press as the pronouncement of a sage. When he
declared in Tonopah during the summer of 1915 that he had
been compelled to corral his colts and calves because in all
his experience in Nevada he had never seen the mountain
lions "so numerous and so daring," the story rumbled far
across the state. Newspapermen glimpsed an exciting biography in the Longstreet saga, though the difficulties posed
by compiling it from scanty sources apparently prevented
them from proceeding with the project. Reporter Elton Garrett observed, "Longstreet's life, could it be compiled, would
make one of the most interesting biographies of western
man." Carl Glasscock, the prime source on Longstreet, called
him "the most perfect typification of the Old West's gunmen
in all the restless camps of the desert's last great mining
excitement."

Among the campfire storytellers, a tendency was developing to connect Longstreet with every dramatic episode
within reach of the imagination. There were those who sol-
emnly swore that Longstreet rode for the Pony Express,
served the Confederacy with Moseby's Raiders, and fought
beside Billy the Kid. Such legends aside, the only story about
his early life that had clearly originated from Longstreet's
own lips concerned a fight with the Cheyenne while he was
traveling with two companions through Wyoming some time
after the Civil War.

The three of them had hobbled their horses and made
camp. Suddenly a storm of Indian arrows and bullets rained
down upon them. One of his companions was killed, the other
badly wounded by an arcing arrow that had flown high in
the air and plummeted down upon him. Among the Indians
was a "pretty fellow" who had oiled his body in preparation
for battle until his skin was so highly polished that it shone.
With great satisfaction, Longstreet recalled shooting this
one "right through the middle" and catching another "right
between the eyes." This halted the Indian rush upon the two

Longstreet (center) with two friends at his mine

embattled white men. The party of warriors withdrew and took cover.

Longstreet thought he knew their strategy: they were watching the hobbled horses, waiting for him to make his move. The instant he approached the horses they would be upon him. Unless he could devise another means of escape, he and his wounded companion would die like antelope trapped in a Cheyenne hunting pit.

While waiting for darkness to fall, Longstreet perfected his plan. Then, ever so silently, he and his friend slipped away while the Indians kept an intent vigil over their hobbled horses. The two of them circled back to the spot where the Indians' own horses were stationed. They stole two, Longstreet cut up his army coat to make bridles, and they made good their escape. Longstreet reckoned that they put nearly forty miles between themselves and the Cheyenne warriors before morning.

Although such lapses from reticence as this reminiscence were exceedingly rare on Longstreet's part, he made news even when he had little to say. His appearance as a witness in the protracted Muddy River water rights litigation in 1917 was covered by the press under the headline "An Old Pioneer Visits Las Vegas." More than two decades after he had casually moved on from the Moapa, his old ranch had been purchased by a California corporation for a price more than forty times greater than Wiser had paid him. The ranch had multiplied in value, not only for its fields of fertile black soil but also for its water right, which the *Las Vegas Age* called "the primary water right in the valley," being the first to be secured on the Muddy after the Mormons departed from the region. Longstreet's testimony, which unfortunately has not been preserved, was essential to the legal decision on water rights in the area because he was believed to be "the only survivor of the band that settled there many years ago." As usual, the local newspaper commented upon the old gentleman's extraordinarily robust appearance: "Not withstanding his half century of life in the wilds, he is still as hale and hearty and as vigorous as in his youthful days."

As long as his remarkable vigor lasted, and that was nearly to the end, Longstreet continued to drive down in the buckboard with Fannie for a few days of roistering with the Ash Meadows crowd. And Mat-oits, the Moon Woman, who Paiute legend says made a homesick visit to her people and bounced over the Indian camp like a great golden bubble, flattening her tribesmen and their dwellings, did not return with more devastating effect than did Longstreet. Once more a piece of canvas was spread upon the ground and the old crowd gathered in a circle, playing cards or the stick game and drinking the good wine brewed in the Pahrump Valley. There they would sit hour after hour, as the days ran on.

Quarrels sparked up, and died, and flared anew when, as George Ishmael put it, they "got up their courage to start out again." After enough wine, every player in the circle became a "mongits," the Nuwuvi word for a drunken man meaning "one who is lost." Once—Ishmael thinks it was around 1916 when he was a teenager—one of these quarrels slid into the danger zone. It was a quarrel over cards, but it somehow also involved Longstreet's half-breed friend Albert Howell, a man of about half Longstreet's age, an argument between Fannie and her sister, who was Howell's wife, and a small Negro boy. Longstreet and Howell were ready to kill each other, but when Longstreet aimed his pistol at Howell, Ishmael swiftly knocked his arm upward and the bullet whistled harmlessly into the air. At Longstreet's advanced time of life and stage of drunkenness, the impulse to kill Howell seems to have guttered out rather easily, yet it appears that he won his point nonetheless. The little Negro boy went to live with Longstreet.

If Longstreet in the last years of his life was less formidable than he used to be, he was still formidable enough to inspire the respect of his contemporaries. According to forest ranger Basil Crane, the region around Longstreet Canyon still abounded with mustangs long after a clean-up effort swept them from the rest of central Nevada because no one had dared to round up wild horses in the vicinity of Longstreet's rifle. Nor did they dare to linger over long with their sheep.

"Wild Indian" Iver, who worked as a buckaroo in the region and was known for a skin "black as the ace of spades," a mane of long, flying hair, and a crazy laugh, used to tell a story about the days when he was herding sheep for William Marsh and John Nay. Marsh was well known in Nye County as a state legislator and one of the original locators of Goldfield; John Nay was Joe's brother. Both men were ranchers with a good deal of land in the area, and they customarily drove their sheep south through the Stone Cabin Valley in the winter, then north again in summer.

On one of these summer drives, Marsh and Nay told "Wild Indian" Iver to water the sheep and make camp at the spring by Longstreet's place. Iver knew that the last part of this order was a dangerous breach of the unwritten code under which Longstreet permitted ranchers making a drive through the valley to use his spring. Although Longstreet was known to detest sheep, as did many old cattlemen of his generation, he allowed the sheepmen to water their animals, provided the pause was brief and the herd was promptly moved along the valley. Making camp at his spring was another matter entirely. "Wild Indian" Iver warned Marsh and Nay, "Jack Longstreet going kill you. He come down hill. He come outa canyon riding sorrel and carrying forty-four. He kill us."

Marsh, a large, heavy, reddish-haired man who boasted of his friendship with Longstreet, made light of this danger. Both he and Nay had a few words to say about how they meant to handle the old man. With considerable misgivings, Iver lit a campfire and set about brewing the coffee. His warning presently proved all too well founded. A big, white-bearded figure came riding through the sagebrush on a sorrel horse and tersely demanded, "What are you doing here?"

The bravado of Marsh and Nay underwent a sudden collapse. "We're just watering, Jack," they murmured meekly. Iver offered Longstreet a cup of coffee.

"Move the sheep. No coffee," said Longstreet. Marsh and Nay hastened to start the herd northward through the valley. When recounting his story in later years, "Wild Indian" Iver used to slyly add, with that crazy laugh of his, "It's the first time I watch two big white men get real small."

The enactment of Prohibition in 1918 brought Longstreet a sideline well suited to his talents and inclinations, as well as to his advanced age. The old frontiersman and former saloonkeeper, who had always enjoyed his liquor, was no more likely to conform to the new law that denied him a drink than to the old law that forbade him to lie with an Indian woman. So when a Tonopah bootlegger with Los Angeles connections proposed setting up a still in Longstreet Canyon and paying Longstreet $500 a month to guard the operation, the offer was accepted. From the bootlegger's point of view, the setup seemed ideal. Longstreet Canyon was too remote to be easily scrutinized by law officers. Even if they should decide to investigate the canyon, they would have to contend with Longstreet's .44.

Nonetheless, as often happens with the best-laid plans, this one went awry. The bootlegger's initial run to Los Angeles with a couple of trucks of illicit liquor must have attracted attention to the operation. When law officers closed in on the canyon shortly afterward, Longstreet was out riding. They were able to split the barrels, pour the liquor over the still, and set it afire without disturbance from a rider on a sorrel horse.

With smoke pluming into the skies above the burning still, the officers would have been wise to close the books on the matter, but they made the mistake of returning the next day with the Nye County district attorney to make certain the operation had been entirely destroyed. This time Longstreet was not out riding. Upon their arrival at his cabin on their way to the charred remains of the still farther up the canyon, he appeared in the doorway with his long-barreled gun and inquired what they were going to do. When they told him they were going in to investigate, he said, "Go ahead, but nobody's coming out."

No one took another step forward. A consensus having very suddenly developed among all present to the effect that this particular operation required no further scrutiny, the law officers beat a hasty retreat down the canyon. Sounding astonished that such things could still happen in the civilized twentieth century, the district attorney later told Tom

The Longstreet Mine in the Monitor Mountains at the peak of operations (Cada C. Boak Collection, Nevada Historical Society)

Clifford, "If we'd gone up, he'd have killed us all." The matter
of bootlegging in Longstreet Canyon was not further pursued.

Riding guard for these bootleggers was, of course, only a
temporary interlude for Longstreet. Most of his time was
spent working the Longstreet mine, with the occasional help
of the Reeds, who held a half-interest in the enterprise. In
1913 Longstreet even temporarily abandoned his buckboard
to make a train trip through Carson City and Reno to raise
capital for developing the mine. Though he still bought and
sold a few claims elsewhere, the Longstreet mine became his
ruling preoccupation. Perhaps the mines worth fortunes that
he had passed over in his earlier days rankled a good deal
more than he cared to admit.

Beneath the tall, conical pinons on the southern side of the
canyon, he built a windowless, dirt-floored dugout of uneven
gray, white, and golden stones, mortared with mud, and

roofed with rough timbers and earth. He began to stay there a good deal of the time. Perhaps he grew fond of this corner of the earth, where a profusion of wild roses sweetened the air in June, birds sang, eagles climbed the air above the sheer mountain wall that closed the canyon in the west, and the wind rushed through the tall pinons with the sound of surf. In the end, by the sheer sweat of his brawny old arms, he had drilled and tunneled 1,400 feet into the mountain, leaving a pile of white tailings high on the slope above the dugout.

Even though no gold or silver of any value was ever taken from the Longstreet mine, these years of hard labor may have contributed to his remarkable good health in old age. Yet it is also possible to see Longstreet's obsession as the last bitter curse of the mine's discoverer, Bob Black: *Let him who took my life waste his own in delving for a treasure he will never find inside the darkness of the earth where I lie.* On evenings when the running footsteps of the dark spirits seem to rustle in the night that races from the mountain to swallow the sunlit valley as a wolf takes his prey, it does not stretch belief over far to think so.

When not working in the mine, Longstreet continued to breed and sell fine horses. Nye County old-timers still recall that when you wanted to buy a top thoroughbred, you went to Longstreet. One of the corollaries to this was that when you loaned a thoroughbred stallion to Longstreet and it was not returned, you abstained from mentioning the matter. On his trips into Tonopah every two or three months to fill the buckboard with supplies and to do some drinking with his friends, progressing along the street from one saloon to the next, Longstreet usually ended at Lee Henderson's Mizpah garage, which doubled as a kind of cattlemen's club where the conversation frequently centered on horses. Henderson, in the phrase of an old cowboy friend, was "always very fond of a well-broke saddle horse, one that's high-falutin', with top manners about him." Much of what he knew about these animals, Henderson had learned as a horsebreaker for

Longstreet, and a strong bond remained between the two of them. "Jack had been a bad man all right," Henderson acknowledged, "but he was straight with his friends, and I liked him."

When cowboys, miners, and prospectors from a hundred miles around gathered to watch the bands, the big parade, and other events at Tonopah's grand Fourth of July celebration, Longstreet still occasionally participated in the horse races. Most often some young cowboy jockeyed a Longstreet horse, but Glasscock wrote of once watching Longstreet ride his own horse (perhaps the one named Woodpecker Junior) to victory in the old men's race. "Good race, Jack," a friend remarked afterward, "but you wouldn't have made it if this pony hadn't been so carefully shod."

"Yeah," said Jack. "Fannie shod that horse. Damn good job too, for a sixty-year-old squaw." This was but one of Longstreet's left-handed compliments to Fannie, who not only shoed horses and waited upon him hand and foot but also cranked the heavy ore buckets to the surface at his mine. Longstreet was said to have remarked that she was "not much of a wife but very good on the windlass."

Besides racing his horses, Longstreet brought a string of mustangs that he had rounded up in the Stone Cabin Valley into Tonopah every Fourth of July and sold them to the children at $5 apiece. Even when there were no mustangs to buy, Longstreet's arrival in town was always a big event to the children. They crowded around, hoping to get close enough to talk to him. Some savored the taste of fear in the nearness of the dangerous man they had heard so many stories about and convinced themselves that he just might "pull a gun out and take a shot at you." Others were awestruck at seeing the living legend so close, so blue-eyed, so broad-shouldered, and so towering tall ("He was someone you really admired," Joe Clifford recalled). Still others, like Alice Lorigan, were warmed by his kindness: "We looked on Longstreet as a hero. We'd all gather around him, and he'd answer so soft-spoken and nice. You'd think he'd be a terrible grouch, but he wasn't." Of course, they all edged as close as they dared, trying to steal a peep at the scarred place under the long hair on the left side of his head.

Implicit in this image of the old man surrounded by children is the emptiness of the log cabin in Windy Canyon, and all the other cabins before it. Small as these cabins were, they were never small enough for just a man and a woman. There was too much space for the unborn son to whom he might have taught riding and the finer points by which to judge a horse and told the secrets that no one was ever to hear, a son who might have given point to his wealth. Longstreet did what he could to fill the places of the children and the grandchildren who would never be. The little Negro boy he had brought north with him from Ash Meadows lived with him for some years. His friends the Myers left their boys with Longstreet and Fannie while they were away, often for weeks at a time.

Of all these desert waifs taken in from the storm, the one that came closest to becoming a child of Longstreet's own was Emma, the Indian girl whom Longstreet and Fannie had raised ever since she was tiny. He came to love her as dearly as though she were his own flesh-and-blood daughter, and she, in turn, called herself by his name instead of her own McClanahan surname, though she was never formally adopted.

After Emma had grown into a striking, exotically beautiful young woman, Longstreet had Lee Henderson fit him out with an old Ford automobile. Longstreet was no great hand at mechanics, never having dealt much with the workings of anything other than guns, and he was far more at ease on the saddle or in the buckboard than in this clanking metal contrivance. The car was for Emma. There, in her fashionable cloche hat and her fur-collared coat, she could ride like the finest of young ladies. He and Fannie had lived lean all their lives and knew no other way. But Emma was different. She

Longstreet, his adopted daughter Emma, his wife Fannie, and an unidentified child at his ranch in the Monitor Montains, probably about 1920 (Nevada State Museum and Historical Society, Las Vegas)

was so young, so affectionate, and so pretty, and she enjoyed these fancy things. Longstreet didn't know a way that the money he packed around in the old suitcase could be better spent.

Fannie, on the other hand, did not hold with spoiling Emma. Her emotions were a good deal more complicated than his. She had scarcely moved into Longstreet's cabin before she had to start sharing him with the little girl, and Emma had not moved on out of their lives like the other children that Longstreet insisted on taking in. Hard as Fannie herself would work in waiting on Longstreet, she drove

The Longstreet ranch in the Monitor Mountains, 1984 (author's photo)

Emma ten times harder ("like a slave," it was said). In Fannie's idea of the natural order, a woman must wait on her husband, the young must wait on the old, and the orphan child with no claims of kin must do even more of the waiting. Yet there was a harder edge to her driving than Emma's lowly place on the ladder-rung of the world required. People remember Fannie being "kind of rough" on Emma, almost as though Longstreet's affection for the girl had made her jealous. There had long been a dark streak, like the black, jagged lightning mark on a Indian bowl, in Fannie's kind of love.

In the 1920s, Longstreet was the last man in the region who still carried a gun on the range. The long-barreled .44 of ancient vintage that he preferred to the modern self-cocking variety was as integral a part of his appearance as the ten-

gallon hat, the red bandanna knotted around his throat, the
Levis, the old work shirt, and the white beard. To Leafy Nay,
its lingering presence was certain proof of his outlaw character ("I never did call him a cowboy, because everyone called
him an outlaw"); others were more interested in the five
notches under the butt. Since the gunfighter tradition, which
Longstreet may or may not have honored, allowed no
notches for Mexicans and Indians, just one of these could be
definitely accounted for—Alexander Dry. What of the other
four? Henderson, who seems to have known the old man as
well as anyone did, observed, "I don't know whether the
notches were for dead men or to improve the grip, or just for
moral effect. Jack would never say. He was no talker."

In the end, though, it was Longstreet's own gun that
wounded him as no adversary had ever succeeded in doing.
He jostled one of his guns while getting out of the buckboard,
sending a bullet into his own armpit and his shoulder. Joe
Nay, hearing of the incident, shook his head sympathetically and remarked to his family, "Poor old Longstreet. Now
he knows what it is to get some hot lead."

Longstreet, for the only time in nearly half a century,
found himself in a white, sterile hospital bed. It did not last
long. A nurse came into his room in the Tonopah hospital
and insisted on washing his face. When she lifted his hair,
exposing the terrible disfigurement that shamed him still,
even after so many years, he rose from his bed and threatened to kill her.

Soon he was back in his mountains. If there were to be any
remedy besides time and space, it would be the Indian kind,
an aromatic poultice of sage leaves boiled over a smoky fire,
and salve from the powdered inner bark of the mountain
mahogany or the sweet, shredded bark of the wild rose. No
more would he submit to being poked at and probed and exposed by alien hands. For all these years, he had known how
he wanted to live. Now he knew how he wanted to die.

The unhealed wound festered long, and the dirty old sling

Longstreet wore around his arm became as familiar a part of his outfit as the bandanna at his throat. He carried on as well as he could, but the man who was once so swift and agile that he could vault into the saddle of his horse without touching a stirrup required a stump to help him mount. The homestead began to show neglect, its fences unmended, its unwatered meadows drying back into wasteland. He agreed to sell the mine to an Oakland syndicate for a large sum.

A heat wave gripped the region in the summer of 1928. On July 25 the man who worked a mine five miles from Windy Canyon grew concerned. Although Longstreet had made it his custom to ride over for a daily visit, three days had passed without a sign of him. He found the old man lying alone, "without any assistance," paralyzed by a stroke that left him unable to move his limbs. Longstreet seemed to recognize his friend, but he was unable to speak.

They brought him into the Mines Hospital in Tonopah. It is uncertain how much he saw or knew of the familiar landmarks on his last passage through the valley, the outcropping of stone just north of Stone Cabin that glows tawny umber above the green-gold rabbitbrush, the rose and gray-green Hot Creek range tumbled like a dissolving sand castle in the distance. His old friends Reed and Henderson stood by his bedside in the hospital. The doctor had told them that he could not last much longer. After all, the man was ninety years old. Those three days without water in the deadly summer heat were more than enough to have killed a younger, lesser man long since, even without the stroke. And yet, somehow, he still lived.

A car was sent to the ranch for Fannie late on the afternoon of the following day. Her absence during the time that he lay stricken has not been satisfactorily explained. Had she turned aside from him, believing, in the Southern Paiute way, that a man grown old and helpless is better left to die? Death songs are made and sung around the campfire when such a one has walked upon the earth so long that his spirit cries "enough" and begs to pass into the other world. If he lingers on too long, a burden to his people, the evil spirits claim him, and he is condemned to wander this world forever as one of them. Was Fannie, in this final, merciless turning away, more Bob Black's sister than Longstreet's wife?

There was to be no leave-taking between the two of them, no resolution through the wordless locking of the dark eyes with the blue. The automobile bringing Fannie from the mountains did not reach Tonopah until after Longstreet died at eleven that night.

Around the wavy line that is the Indian sign for the ebb and flow of life, death had closed the circle.

Notes

The numerous versions of the Breyfogle story include those of Belden, *Mines of Death Valley*, 21-25; J. Frank Dobie, *Coronado's Children*, (New York: Literary Guild, 1931), 208-15; Coolidge, *Death Valley Prospectors*, 61-76; William A. Chalfant, *Death Valley: The Facts*, 3rd ed. (Palo Alto: Stanford University Press, 1930), 47-50; and the definitive discussion in Lingenfelter, *Death Valley & the Amargosa*, 73-79. Longstreet's search for the lost Breyfogle was reported in the *Carson City Daily Appeal*, April 7, 1915.

This chapter has drawn on the recollections of Marguerite Boscovich (March 31, 1983), Joseph Clifford, Helen Falani (August 1981), Buster Fillippini, Dennis Hill (March 31, 1983), George Ishmael, Olephia King, Pete Peterson, Solon Terrell (August 10, 1983), Austin Wardle, Robert Williams (August 1981), and others who prefer not to be mentioned. Anecdotes on Longstreet are recounted in Basil K. Crane, *Dust from an Alkali Flat* (Reno: University of Nevada Press, 1984), 64, 144-47; the *Tonopah Bonanza*, March 18, 1907; the *Churchill County Eagle*, August 7, 1915; and the *Las Vegas Age*, February 18, 1911, January 25, 1913, and August 18, 1917. On Leland F. ("Lee") Henderson, see Glasscock, *Gold in Them Hills*, 215-16. Percy Train, James R. Heinrichs, and W. Andrew Archer discuss Indian herbal remedies in "Medicinal Uses of Plants by Indian Tribes of Nevada," in David A. Horr, ed., *Paiute Indians*, vol. 4

in the Garland American Indian Ethnohistory Series (New York: Garland Publishing, 1974).

On Longstreet's death, see his death certificate (Section of Vital Statistics, Nevada Division of Health, Carson City) and his obituaries in the *Tonopah Mining Reporter*, July 28, 1928, the *Tonopah Daily Times*, July 27, 1928, the *Tonopah Bonanza*, July 27, 1928, and the *Las Vegas Review*, July 30, 1928.

9
Belmont

Longstreet had wanted to be as isolated from the busy, civilized world of other men in death as he had been in life. The final resting place he mentioned to newspaperman Eli Norton Richardson shortly before he died was the lonely mountainside above his ranch. Nonetheless, on July 30, 1928, his family and friends gave him a conventional burial in the graveyard in the lee of the craggy hill southeast of Belmont. He was hailed in newspaper obituaries and subsequent retrospectives as the last of the desert frontiersmen, the stranger with a "halo of mystery" who had spent his life "roaming the West when there was a West," the survivor of dangerous times when a man was compelled to "think fast, shoot first, and argue the case afterwards."

Slight acquaintances hastily elevated themselves to boon companions. "There are only a few of us left," newspaperman William W. Booth wrote in a letter informing Longstreet's former attorney George Bartlett of his death. In this, Booth presumed too much. It is doubtful that any of the young men who came to Tonopah at the turn of the century really belonged in Longstreet's company. The ones who did, the other old frontiersmen, had died long before, leaving him to live on alone beyond his time, increasingly a stranger in the alien world of the twentieth century.

The estate remained to be settled, not without a little squabbling between Fannie and Emma. Though Longstreet had apparently read the signs in his failing body and had at last decided to make a will, he had not gotten further than writing a note saying he wanted Fannie to receive a small monthly allotment for the remainder of her lifetime. He wanted Henderson, his friend and former horse breaker, to administer the estate, or what remained of it. Nearly all the money in the old suitcase had gone one way or another, $5,000 of it lent to Bartlett, who found himself in financial exigencies despite his position as a highly respected judge in Reno, far removed from the days when he came to Tonopah as a young man to seek "my only salvation" and helped to defend Longstreet after the gunfight with the Cliffords. Although the Bartlett note was never repaid, other funds—the sale of the ranch to John Nay for a small sum, the disposal of the cattle and horses, a payment on the mine by the Golden Lion syndicate, and other bits and pieces—added together made enough for Fannie.

Emma, who had received nothing, asked for $500 to take a beautician's course in Los Angeles. Fannie would agree only if Emma would promise to take care of her; this Emma refused, having already spent enough years waiting on Fannie and receiving the sharp side of her tongue. Claiming payment for the use of her horses over an eight-year period, Emma sued the estate and eventually received enough money in settlement for her training course. She managed to move upward from house cleaning, the usual occupation for an Indian woman, to become a beautician before she died in Tonopah while still young.

Fannie returned to her old home in Ash Meadows and soon found that she had more kin than she had counted on. At first, coming back as a respected widow to the tribe that had once cast out her renegade brother may have seemed a balm to family pride. Not for her the death by slow starvation to avoid burdening her people, in the way of the Indian women of an earlier day. Fannie, with her monthly allotment, was

wealthy by the standards of Ash Meadows, so wealthy that
Henderson began receiving letters from Indians all around
the country who claimed an interest in the Longstreet estate.
Without Longstreet at her side to hold them at bay, Fannie
soon found the press of the crowd more than she could bear.
As Henderson phrased it, "The Indians all moved in and
thought she had a million dollars." After a few months of
this, Fannie fled north. She refused to return to the ranch in
Windy Canyon, saying she would have nothing further to do
with it. Henderson was hard put to dissuade her from burning the place, as the Indians have traditionally done with the
dwellings of their dead.

In the belief of Fannie's people, the spirits of the dead make
the passage to Na-gun-tu-weap, a beautiful valley of eternal
abundance, provided they are valiant enough to traverse a
gloomy underground cavern resounding with the hideous
growls of invisible beasts and the screeches of monstrous
birds and to cross a treacherous narrow bridge above a
yawning chasm. That the ghost of the formidable Longstreet
would quail before the perils of this hellish journey was
surely inconceivable to Fannie, if she saw him as enough an
Indian for Na-gun-tu-weap. Yet he had lived so long, far
beyond the age when the greatest chieftains sought death
lest their spirits be condemned to wander the earth forever as
cowardly ghosts. Perhaps his spirit walked the mountains
still, angry with the wife who had abandoned him to lie three
days in his dying. Salvation lay in the ways of her fathers.
For generations the Southern Paiutes had taught their children that a dead man's dwelling must be consumed by fire
lest his ghost return.

Though Henderson eventually convinced Fannie that the
ranch must not be burned because it was about to be sold, she
was too much an Indian to return to a dead man's hearth.
Instead she camped at the mine in Longstreet Canyon. It
was there, in the snows of a December storm, that a rescue

party found her pinioned like a helpless moth beneath her collapsed tent. After that she lived most of the time in a small cabin behind Henderson's Mizpah garage in Tonopah.

On the night of May 11, 1931, a strange glow illuminated Mt. Oddie at the northeastern side of town. An overturned lamp had showered Fannie with burning oil and set the cabin on fire. By the time Henderson found Fannie moaning near the back porch, dragged her out of the burning cabin, and rolled her small body in a carpet to extinguish her flaming clothes, she was already terribly burned. Death relieved her sufferings an hour later. Her tombstone was placed in the Belmont cemetery beside Longstreet's, in the open space to the right of the gate, where the eye travels on without obstruction beyond the two identical hoops of low, polished stone into the wide, sage-covered expanse of the Monitor Valley and the far mountains.

Most of the places that Longstreet knew in the restless rovings of nearly half a century remain for all to see. The Moapa fields that were Longstreet's are still good fertile farmland, but the St. Thomas saloon where Longstreet and Alexander Dry once drank before riding north together to their deadly encounter at the river crossing disappeared for years beneath the dammed swell of the Colorado. Since the construction of Glen Canyon Dam, however, the indigo waters of Lake Mead have receded enough to expose once more the ruined foundations of the old settlement.

Along the Amargosa the future wavers uneasily between development into farms and homesites, and conservation intended to preserve the remarkable springs and the rare desert pupfish. The survival of these tiny, silvery blue fish in the increasing salinity and warm temperatures of an ever more restricted environment, together with the extraordinary speed of their evolution, holds considerable interest for modern scientists. The Devil's Hole pupfish, the most isolated among them, are found nowhere else on earth except in a single shallow pool at the mouth of a tiny crevice. These fish have evolved into a new species, probably even a new genus, within only ten or twenty thousand years—a mere snap of the fingers in evolutionary time. Devil's Hole, their habitat, has already been designated a national monument, an Ash Meadows National Wildlife Refuge has been created to preserve animals and plants unique to the area, and the Nature Conservancy has been endeavoring to acquire other springs before real estate operations have irrevocably determined the future of the region.

South of Ash Meadows, where Longstreet and the Indian trackers trailed the blood-spattered Jim Boone, Pahrump has already gone in the direction of development. Quarter-acre homesites are offered for sale, a shopping mall and country club have been constructed, and sprinklers turn busily on the manicured greens of the new golf course.

At Ash Meadows the onward march of progress has thus far been more erratic. Longstreet's stone cabin still stands beside the aquamarine pool in the white and gold landscape of dried grass and mineral-encrusted earth, but subsequent owners have leveled the bluff behind it, scraping away the mesquite thicket, smashing down the rear of the cabin, and obliterating any corrals or outbuildings in its vicinity. The old cabin is now within the domain of a large and well-kept ranch run with an efficiency neither practiced nor much admired by the shiftless squaw men of the last century. Mining in an industrious mode that parallels the new ranching is also proceeding nearby. In place of the circle of Indian gamblers whiling away the long, sunny afternoons, miners housed in neat rows of trailers work the clay and borax deposits on the western side of the Meadows.

Even though the respectable world has made some encroachments and the local population no longer consists of outlaw drifters who fight and kill, the settlement north of Shadow Mountain remains a long way from Sun City. For some years it has been well known for its bordello, which a faithful clientele, recently said to be supplemented by Japanese tourists, considered well worth the trip of more than eighty miles from Las Vegas. A trace of the acrid flavor of the old Ash Meadows, like alkali dust on the tongue, can occasionally be detected while approaching a shanty along a path strewn with the severed heads of goats or standing in the sun beside the vermeil brilliance of a fallen cottonwood amidst the yapping of innumerable dogs and listening to their owner's polemics concerning her stolen herd of mustangs. A real enemy is still called a "horse thief" by some of the older residents.

North of Ash Meadows a large portion of the Unexplored Desert that Longstreet signposted for those to follow lies inside the Las Vegas Bombing and Gunnery Range, once more forbidden ground, now for a different reason. Even farther north, Tonopah has undergone fewer changes than many of the now-abandoned ghost towns that Longstreet frequented. The original mines have fallen silent for years and abandoned tailings dot the hillsides. But the dice continue to roll, the glasses clink, and Tonopah lives on as the lively supply center to the miners and ranchers of a vast region.

The Kawich and the Stone Cabin Valley remain much as they were in the days when sheepmen kept their herds moving smartly through the valley from fear of a rider on a sorrel horse. While Golden Arrow has lately undergone a minor revival during which burly young men in trailers and a booted girl in a gypsy scarf worked the mines at the phantom town of Longstreet, nothing but an old wooden headframe and a rusted barrel remain to mark the site today. Antelope still bound across the green-gold rabbitbrush of Cactus Flat; small bands of mustangs, black, white, and chestnut, like those Longstreet sold to the children on Fourth of July, still pause to regard the intruder, then gallop away in Indian file along their narrow trails into the hills. From the heights near Red Rock Ranch, the winking diamond lights of Goldfield

are now visible more than forty miles away, where Longstreet in 1899 saw only the clear desert night and perhaps the
silver smear of a meteor. Yet even today, it is possible, in the
gully where Longstreet and the Cliffords fought their gun
battle, to die alone with the terrifying knowledge that days,
perhaps weeks, may elapse before another human being will
pass within miles of the place. Red Rock Ranch remains very
far beyond the pale.

No one lives in Windy Canyon any longer, or works the
Longstreet mine. The Golden Lion syndicate claimed at one
point to have spent $100,000 developing it, and Crown Reef
Consolidated, capitalized at more than $1,000,000, also at-
tempted to exploit the claims, but Bob Black's last bitter joke
held true to the end: no ore of real value was ever taken from
the mine. Farther south the Cliffords continue to ranch the
Stone Cabin Valley, their herds of cattle fanning far over the
range.

During the atomic bomb tests on the Las Vegas range, the
dusty fallout sometimes sifted so thickly over the ranch that
it was impossible to see fifty feet. The heavy stone blocks in
Stone Cabin, which had stood since settlers first came to the
valley, tumbled down in the shock wave, dogs died, the backs
of horses blistered, and lesions like burns appeared on the
skins of the Cliffords. They stayed on, through the bomb
tests and through the recent threat of losing their lands to the
proposed MX missile range, as they have stayed through the
hardships of a century, believing, in the words of Joe Clifford, "If they take us out, they're going to have to take us out
the hard way." The old frontiersman with whom the Cliffords had finally made their peace would have understood.

Across the peaks of the Monitor range in Belmont, pigeons
roost in the eaves of the abandoned red brick courthouse
where Longstreet twice stood trial. On a street of ruined gray
stone walls, the old Cosmoplitan Saloon stands yet, its weath-
ered boards peeling away from their frames, the front porch
leaning crazily to one side, the sky showing blue through a

latticework of holes in the roof. A handful of people still live in Belmont or spend weekends there, and a new home or two has sprouted on the hillsides, but Belmont's remoteness, coupled with the absence of such amenities as electricity, telephones, mail delivery, and running water, have thus far held development of the golf course and shopping mall variety at bay. The slow process of blowing down and crumbling away that had already commenced when Longstreet rode north from Ash Meadows continues in Belmont today.

In the Belmont graveyard, after a summer rain, the sage and juniper smell as sweet as flowers. Absorbed moisture blackens the old wooden crosses, fences, and fallen monuments so that they look charred by fire. The trunk of the aged, bent juniper is bowed in a smooth curve, and the ground under the pinons is cobbled with many seasons of cones. Someone who still remembers has left white plastic daisies on the graves of Longstreet and Fannie; shiny shards from the plastic flowers of other years lie scattered around the two low stone markers. His reads "John Longstreet 1834–1928." The date of death may be the only accurate part of this inscription: the first and middle names he invariably gave were Andrew Jackson, no evidence suggesting that he was born in 1834 has as yet been uncovered, and his true last name remains in doubt. If he was in actuality a close relative of Confederate General James Longstreet, as many of his contemporaries believed, he was a member of one of America's oldest and most distinguished families. Yet Andrew Jackson Longstreet nowhere appears in the genealogy of the Southern branch of the Longstreet family, nor in the extensive records of Louisiana and Kentucky, the states variously given as his birthplace.

Longstreet leaves the genealogists baffled and defeated in his wake like confounded trackers—perhaps by bequeathing them a false trail. As. C. L. Sonnichsen has written of another elusive figure, there was a certain type of man in the remoter reaches of the West who did not always "answer to

Longstreet's tombstone in the Belmont cemetery, 1983 (author's photo)

the name he was known by." Andrew Jackson, the idol of the Western frontier and the Battle of New Orleans, and General Longstreet, the hero of the southwestern Confederacy, combine into a name that is almost too mythic to credit. It is the kind of name that a fugitive born on the frontier, perhaps an ex-Confederate soldier, might choose on impulse, but there is no anonymity about it, no canny effort at concealment with the common kind of John Doe name that will pass unnoticed in a crowd. If it was a name not given but chosen, it was chosen by a man proud and defiant enough to fly his heroes like a banner over his second life with the certainty that none would dare to question him too closely.

Some of the legends surrounding him remain as dubious as his name. Did he really fight for the Confederacy with Mose-

by's Raiders? It cannot be denied that the shoe of the guer-
rilla fits him well. Harrying the Union encampments and
supply lines by day and by night, riding swiftly on to the next
skirmish, looting, stealing horses for the Confederate troops,
and living off the land—all would have suited him far better
than the grinding discipline of the regular army. Yet the
name of Andrew Jackson Longstreet is conspicuously absent from the Confederate Consolidated Military Service Index, as is that of any Longstreet who cannot be otherwise
accounted for.

Was he a Pony Express rider? While Longstreet's name is
not listed among the known Express riders, not everyone
rode under his own name, the company kept few records during its brief existence from 1860 through 1861, and the lists
are not considered definitive. He certainly had the youth, the
horsemanship, and the nerve of a typical Pony Express rider,
and certain bonus abilities with a gun that would have
served the Express company well. Possibly he came forward,
unlisted and unmentioned, to take the place of a missing or
overly anxious rider in some frontier emergency. It is also not
improbable that if Longstreet had any real connection with
the early western mail service, it was as a shotgun messenger, the same capacity in which he rode for the Tonopah
and Goldfield stages in his old age, and it was with another
company than the Pony Express, perhaps in the Arizona territory where he first appeared in 1880. Where Longstreet is
concerned, truth has a way of dissolving into legend, and legend into truth.

Longstreet's own stories about himself made mention of
Montana and Wyoming, suggesting a northerly route westward from Kentucky and Arkansas, never involving Texas.
Yet most old-timers believe that Longstreet spent his youth
in Texas and suffered his disfigurement in that state. Texas
to New Mexico to Arizona would have been a natural path
west for a young man born in Louisiana, or perhaps a natural escape route, after the 1876 crackdown by the Texas

Rangers forced a host of outlaws to flee Texas not long before
the first appearance of the man calling himself Longstreet in
the Lost Basin country. Along the way, the Longstreet name
turns up a time or two in Apacheria, and it is suggestive that
the Apaches were prone to choose the surnames of white men
they knew and respected. It is also curious that something
about Longstreet's appearance and bearing led others to
mistake him occasionally not simply for an Indian but for a
half-breed Apache.

No mention of Texas or the Apache country can be traced
to Longstreet's lips, but that may have been a necessary dis-
cretion. It is conceivable that a wanted man might have
found it wise to transpose some incidents from Texas to locales farther north, and there were signs that Longstreet was
in that category. More than his reticence, his telltale skill
with guns, and his affinity for lonely places tended to support the theory that he was a man on the run. His extremely
suspicious behavior toward strangers also hinted at precautions greater than natural prudence would dictate, perhaps
the kind of precautions likely to be taken by someone with
the uneasy expectation that his violent past would one day
catch up with him.

In the apparent hope that Longstreet might be inclined to
reveal the truth before he died, newspaperman Richardson
journeyed out from Tonopah to visit him at his ranch not
long before his fatal stroke. Richardson was convinced that
Longstreet's life on the desert could be "woven into a whole
library of wild west tales, more colorful, more thrilling and
more true than the present day 'make-believes' shown on the
silver screen," if the old man could only be persuaded to talk.
Even at ninety, with the bullet wound festering in his
shoulder and his strength failing, Longstreet harbored no
such inclination. He tossed Richardson a brief yarn, like a
hush puppy to a hound, and told the journalist with firm fi-
nality that he had written out the story of his life but did not
"intend it shall be printed" until after his death.

Possibly that was a civil means of cutting off Richardson's questions, since no manuscript written by Longstreet has come to light. He kept his secrets to the grave, and beyond. Yet the essential truth about him could not be so easily concealed. We know him over forty-eight years, a span so long as to encompass a second lifetime. We will have to imagine the first.

Notes

On Longstreet's obituaries and estate matters, see the probate records in the Nye County courthouse, Tonopah; William W. Booth to George A. Bartlett, July 27, 1928; and the financial records in the George A. Bartlett Papers, Special Collections, University Libraries, University of Nevada, Reno; Fannie Longstreet's obituary in the *Nevada State Journal*, May 14, 1931, p. 8; and undated clippings, Longstreet file, Central Nevada Newspapers, Inc., Tonopah. The main oral source was Alice Lorigan.

Recent developments in St. Thomas and Belmont are described in Corbett, "Settling the Muddy River Valley," 150, and the *Gazette-Journal (Reno Gazette-Journal),* September 20, 1981, pp. 1E, 3E.

Bibliography

Books

Angel, Myron, ed. *History of Nevada.* Oakland, Calif.: Thompson & West, 1881.

Bancroft, Hubert H. *History of Nevada 1540-1898.* San Francisco: The History Company, 1890.

Beatty, Bessie. *Who's Who in Nevada.* Los Angeles: Home Printing, 1907.

Belden, L. Burr. *Mines of Death Valley.* Glendale, Calif.: La Siesta Press, 1976.

Bloss, Roy S. *Pony Express—The Great Gamble.* Berkeley: Howell-North, 1959.

Caruthers, William. *Loafing Along Death Valley Trails.* Pomona, Calif.: P-B Press, 1951.

Chalfant, William A. *Death Valley: The Facts.* 3rd ed. Palo Alto: Stanford University Press, 1930.

Chan, Loren B. *Sagebrush Statesman: Tasker L. Oddie of Neveda.* Reno: University of Nevada Press, 1973.

Coolidge, Dane. *Death Valley Prospectors.* New York: Dutton, 1937.

Crane, Basil K. *Dust from an Alkali Flat.* Reno: University of Nevada Press, 1984.

Davis, Sam P., ed. *The History of Nevada.* 2 vols. Reno and Los Angeles: Elms Publishing, 1913.

Dictionary of American Biography. New York: Charles Scribner's Sons, 1933.

Dobie, J. Frank. *Coronado's Children.* New York: Literary Guild, 1931.

Fowler, Don D., and Catherine S. Fowler, eds. *Anthropology of the*

Numa: John Wesley Powell's Manuscripts on the Numic Peoples of Western North America, 1868-1880. Washington, D.C.: Smithsonian Institution Press, 1971.

Gilbert, Bil. *Westering Man: The Life of Joseph Walker.* New York: Atheneum, 1983.

Glasscock, Carl B. *Gold in Them Hills.* New York: Grossett & Dunlap, 1932.

_____. *Here's Death Valley.* New York: Bobbs-Merrill, 1940.

Hafner, Arabell L., ed. *One Hundred Years on the Muddy.* Springville, Utah: Art City Publishing, 1967.

Hinton, Richard J. *The Handbook to Arizona: Its Resources, History, Towns, Mines, Ruins, and Scenery.* Glorieta, N. Mex.: Rio Grande Press, 1878.

Hopkins, Sarah Winnemucca. *Life Among the Piutes: Their Wrongs and Claims.* Bishop, Calif.: Sierra Media, 1969; reproduction of 1883 edition.

Horr, David A., ed. *Paiute Indians.* Vol. 4 in the Garland American Indian Ethnohistory Series. New York: Garland Publishing, 1974.

Inter-Tribal Council of Nevada. *Nuwuvi: A Southern Paiute History.* Reno: Inter-Tribal Council of Nevada, 1976.

Israel, Fred L. *Nevada's Key Pittman.* Lincoln: University of Nebraska Press, 1963.

Jones, Virgil C. *Gray Ghosts and Rebel Raiders.* New York: Henry Holt, 1956.

Lee, Bourke. *Death Valley.* New York: Macmillan, 1930.

Leopold, A. Starker. *The Desert.* New York: Time-Life Books, 1969.

Lingenfelter, Richard E. *Death Valley & the Amargosa: A Land of Illusion.* Berkeley and Los Angeles: University of California Press, 1986.

Mayes, Edward. *Genealogy of the Family of Longstreet.* N.p.: 1893.

McGrath, Roger D. *Gunfighters, Highwaymen, & Vigilantes:* Violence on the Frontier. Berkeley and Los Angeles: University of California Press, 1984.

Muir, John. *Steep Trails.* New York: Houghton Mifflin, 1918.

Nathan, M. C., and W. S. Boggs. *The Pony Express.* New York: Collectors' Club, 1962.

Paher, Stanley W. *Nevada Ghost Towns and Mining Camps.* Berkeley: Howell-North Books, 1970.

Palmer, William R. *Pahute Indian Legends*. Salt Lake City: Deseret Book Publishers, 1946.

Sadovich, Maryellen V. *Your Guide to Southern Nevada*. Carson City: Nevada Historical Society Guide Book Series, 1976.

Shamberger, Hugh A. *Silver Peak*. Carson City: Nevada Historical Press, 1976.

Smith, Waddell F., ed. *The Story of the Pony Express*. San Rafael, Calif.: Pony Express History and Art Gallery, 1964.

Soltz, David L., and Robert J. Naiman. *The Natural History of Native Fishes in the Death Valley System*. Natural History Museum of Los Angeles in Conjunction with the Death Valley Natural History Association, 1978.

Spears, John R. *Illustrated Sketches of Death Valley and Other Borax Deserts of the Pacific Coast*. Chicago and New York: Rand McNally, 1892.

Sonnichsen, C. L. *Outlaw: Bill Mitchell alias Baldy Russell, His Life and Times*. Denver: Sage Books, 1965.

Trenholm, Virginia C., and Maurine Carley. *The Shoshonis: Sentinels to the Rockies*. Norman: University of Oklahoma Press, 1964.

Webber, C. W. *Tales of the Southern Border*. Philadelphia: Lippincott, 1887.

Wheeler, George M. *Preliminary Report Concerning Explorations and Surveys Principally in Nevada and Arizona*. Washington, D.C.: Government Printing Office, 1872.

Zanjani, Sally, and Guy L. Rocha. *The Ignoble Conspiracy: Radicalism on Trial in Nevada*. Reno: University of Nevada Press, 1986.

Articles

Calloway, Colin G. "Neither White nor Red: White Renegades on the American Indian Frontier." *Western Historical Quarterly* 17 (January 1986): 43–66.

Corbett, Pearson S. "Settling the Muddy River Valley." *Nevada Historical Society Quarterly* 18 (Fall 1975): 141–51.

Earl, Phillip I. "Murder Helped Boost Fortunes." *Apple Tree*, February 1, 1981.

Garrett, Elton. "Nuggets of Boulder Color." *Las Vegas Review-Journal*, February 23, 1933.

_____. "Nuggets of Nevada Color." *Tonopah, Nevada, Mining Record Reporter*, April 25, 1931.

Ingalls, G. W. "Indians of Nevada," in *The History of Nevada*, vol. 1, edited by Sam P. Davis (Reno and Los Angeles: Elms Publishing, 1913): 20–189.

Kosso, Lenore M. "Yugoslavs in Nevada, Part I." *Nevada Historical Society Quarterly* 28 (Summer 1985): 69–89.

Lenon, Robert. "The Mines of Gold Basin: A Report of 1883." *Journal of Arizona History* 8 (1967): 256–68.

Lewis, Georgia. "Jack Longstreet." *The Nevadan* (May 18, 1969): 2, 4–5.

Mason, Dorothy, and Allen Metscher. "The Killing of Sheriff Logan." *Central Nevada's Glorious Past* 3 (November 1980).

Metz, Henry. "Letter." *Belmont Courier*, May 9, 1891.

Morse, L. C. "Letter." *Belmont Courier*, August 1, 1891.

Riggs, John L. "The Reign of Violence in El Dorado Canyon." *Third Biennial Report of the Nevada Historical Society, 1911-1912* (Carson City: State Printing Office, 1913): 95–107.

Sadovich, Maryellen V. "James Bernard Wilson—Forgotten Pioneer." *The West* 9 (October 1968): 38–39, 64–66.

Townley, Carrie M. "Helen J. Stewart: First Lady of Las Vegas." *Nevada Historical Quarterly* 16 (Winter 1973): 215–44; 17 (Spring 1974): 2–32.

Townley, John M. "El Dorado Canyon and Searchlight Mining Districts." *Nevada Historical Society Quarterly* 11 (Spring 1968): 5–19.

Train, Percy, James R. Heinrichs, and W. Andrew Archer. "Medicinal Uses of Plants by Indian Tribes of Nevada," in *Paiute Indians*, edited by David A. Horr, vol. 4 in the Garland American Indian Ethnohistory Series. New York: Garland Publishing, 1974: 53-257.

Wash-Pickett, Evelyne. "Tasker Oddie in Belmont." *Nevada Historical Society Quarterly* 29 (Summer 1986): 89–108.

White, Harsha. "Letter." *Belmont Courier*, September 26, 1891.

Newspapers

Alta Arizona
Belmont Courier
Carson City Daily Appeal
Carson City Daily News
Chloride Belt (Candelaria)
Churchill County Eagle
Goldfield Daily News
Goldfield Weekly News
Goldfield Daily Tribune
Goldfield Review
Inyo Independent
Inyo Register
Las Vegas Age
Las Vegas Review-Journal
Manhattan Mail (Nevada)
Nevada State Journal; Reno Gazette-Journal
Pioche Record
Reveille (Austin, Nevada)
Salt Lake City Tribune
San Francisco Examiner
Tonopah Bonanza; Tonopah Times-Bonanza
Tonopah Mining Reporter; Tonopah, Nevada, Mining Record
Walker Lake Bulletin (Hawthorne)

Documents and Unpublished Manuscripts

"Annual Report of the Attorney General of the State of Nevada 1895." *Appendix to the Journals of the Senate and Assembly, 1897.*

Atkins, J. D. C., Commissioner of Indian Affairs, to Special Indian Agent Henry S. Welton, September 20 and 24, 1887, National Archives, Washington, D.C.

Bartlett, George A. Papers. Special Collections, University Libraries, University of Nevada, Reno.

Bradfute, W. R., Moapa Reservation Resident Farmer, to Nevada

Indian Agent W. D. Gibson, June 11, 1887, National Archives, Washington, D.C.

_____. Deposition, October 29, 1887, enclosed with Welton to Commissioner, November 3, 1887, National Archives, Washington, D.C.

Breen, Richard. Probate file, 1900–1902, Nye County courthouse, Tonopah, Nevada.

(Acting) Commissioner of Indian Affairs to Secretary of the Interior, July 13, 1887, National Archives, Washington, D.C.

_____ to Special Indian Agent Henry S. Welton, October 24, 1887, National Archives, Washington, D.C.

Gibson, W. D., Nevada Indian Agent, to J. D. C. Atkins, Commissioner of Indian Affairs, June 27, 1887, National Archives, Washington, D.C.

Index to Mining Claims, Mohave County courthouse, Kingman, Arizona.

Kensler, Charles D. "Survey of Historic Structures: Southern Nevada and Death Valley." Prepared for U.S. Department of Energy, Nevada Operations Office by URS/John S. Blume & Associates, 1982. Nevada Historical Society, Reno.

Kiel, E. B. Deposition, December 8, 1887, enclosed with Welton to Commissioner, December 28, 1887, National Archives, Washington, D.C.

King, Olephia. "Dust and Desire, Laughter and Tears: Recollections of a Nevada Pioneer Cowgirl and Poet." Reno: University of Nevada Oral History Project, 1978–1980.

Longstreet, A. J., to Nevada Indian Agent W. D. Gibson, June 20, 1887, National Archives, Washington, D.C.

_____ to Secretary of the Interior, June 26, 1887, National Archives, Washington, D.C.

_____. Probate file, 1928–1929. Nye County courthouse, Tonopah, Nevada.

Miller, Thomas W. "Memoirs of Thomas Woodnut Miller, a Public Spirited Citizen of Delaware and Nevada." Reno: University of Nevada Oral History Project, 1965.

Oddie, Tasker L. Papers. Nevada Historical Society, Reno.

Pittman, Key. Papers. Library of Congress, Washington, D.C.

(Acting) Secretary of the Interior to Commissioner of Indian Affairs, September 21, 1887. National Archives, Washington, D.C.

Segmiller, George. Deposition, December 12, 1887, enclosed with Welton to Commissioner, December 28, 1887. National Archives, Washington, D.C.

Welton, Henry S., Special Indian Agent, to Commissioner of Indian Affairs, November 3 and 24 and December 28, 1887. National Archives, Washington, D.C.

Wilson, James B. Papers. Special Collections, University Libraries, University of Nevada, Las Vegas.

Oral Interviews

Beatty, Montillious M. November 1, 1968, taped interview, Nevada Historical Society, Reno.

Boscovich, Marguerite. March 31, 1983 (telephone).

Clifford, Joseph. August 1980, August 1981.

DeHart, Sonia. August 1981.

Falani, Helen. August 1981.

Fillippini, Buster. March 31, 1983.

Hill, Dennis. March 31, 1983.

Ishmael, George. March 1, 1983.

King, Olephia. August 20, 1982.

Lorigan, Alice. March 31, 1983.

Petersen, Pete. February 20, 1982.

Rooker, Noreen. February 20, 1982.

Terrell, Solon. August 10, 1983 (telephone).

Wardle, Austin. March 30, 1983.

Williams, Robert. August 1981.

Index

Vintage West Series
Quality Paperback Reprints

Report of Explorations Across the Great Basin . . . in 1859
Captain James H. Simpson

An Editor on the Comstock Lode
Wells Drury

Frémont: Explorer for a Restless Nation
Ferol Egan

Sand in a Whirlwind: The Paiute Indian War of 1860
Ferol Egan

The Town That Died Laughing: The Story of Austin, Nevada
Oscar Lewis

Wells, Fargo Detective: A Biography of James B. Hume
Richard Dillon

Sierra-Nevada Lakes
George and Bliss Hinkle

Exploring the Great Basin
Gloria Griffen Cline

High Sierra Country
Oscar Lewis

I Remember Christine
Oscar Lewis

Sagebrush Trilogy:
Idah Meacham Strobridge and Her Works
Idah Meacham Strobridge

Lady in Boomtown:
Miners and Manners on the Nevada Frontier
Mrs. Hugh Brown

The WPA Guide to 1930s Nevada
the Nevada Writers' Project of the WPA

A Kid on the Comstock:
Reminiscences of a Virginia City Childhood
John Taylor Waldorf

The Story of the Mine:
As Illustrated by the Great Comstock Lode of Nevada
Charles Howard Shinn

Karnee: A Paiute Narrative
Lalla Scott

Will James: The Last Cowboy Legend
Anthony Amaral

The Legend of Grizzly Adams:
California's Greatest Mountain Man
Richard Dillon

Jack Longstreet: Last of the Desert Frontiersmen
Sally Zanjani